"When it comes to finding kind companions on the road to unhurried transformation, I can't think of two people I trust more than Gem and Alan Fadling. For years they've taught me more about what it means to live life deep in the kingdom of God, and now *What Does Your Soul Love?* is not only a transformational question it's also a compelling, life-changing book."

Emily P. Freeman, author of *Simply Tuesday* and *The Next Right Thing*

"In this grounded and thought-provoking book you will be guided to wake up from what is keeping you from living an abundant life. Time is short, and we owe it to ourselves, our community, and our planet to do the important inner work Gem and Alan propose. Read this book and prepare to be changed."

Phileena Heuertz, author of *Mindful Silence* and *Pilgrimage of a Soul*, founding partner of Gravity: A Center for Contemplative Activism

"In this book, Gem and Alan Fadling offer eight seminal questions—power tools, really—that have potential to drill down through the surface of your life into the core of your being. It's in this realm of your inner life, they assure you, that transformation begins. If you've ever wondered how change really happens, *What Does Your Soul Love?* will show you, most poignantly, through the Fadlings' willingness to tell their own vulnerable stories of saying yes to God's transforming love and work. We highly recommend it!"

Beth Booram and David Booram, cofounders of Fall Creek Abbey, spiritual directors, and authors of *When Faith Becomes Sight*

"As I read through this deep and insightful book *What Does Your Soul Love?*, I felt as though I was in a safe space, with deeply kind and wise spiritual directors, gently nudging me to peer into places where I had been afraid to look, to embrace my vulnerability and not run from it, and to place my trust in a God who loves me and longs for my good more than I do for myself. This book is a gift. Thank you Gem and Alan."

James Bryan Smith, author of *The Good and Beautiful God*

"The honest questions and vulnerable answers tucked into the pages of *What Does Your Soul Love?* by Gem and Alan Fadling makes this not only a timely but also a timeless testament to hope. These fresh and accessible confessions are invitations for all of us to move into a more practice-based spirituality—a credible and rooted spirituality that will only foster a more faithful and faith-filled life."

Christopher L. Heuertz, author of *The Sacred Enneagram*

"In an age of frenetic activity and endless surface distractions, Gem and Alan provide just what we need: significant and incisive questions to slow us down enough to reflect and ponder. Their questions, along with their matchless wisdom, engaging stories, practical exercises, and creative spiritual practices, seek to soothe the soul and point us to Jesus. This is more than a book; it's a practical manual to cultivate a with-God life. I'll be referring back to these questions time and time again. I'm confident you will too."

J.R. Briggs, founder of Kairos Partnerships, author of *Fail: Finding Hope in the Midst of Ministry Failure*

"Alan and Gem Fadling are trustworthy guides in the journey of spiritual formation, not only because they have set their minds and hearts on seeking the kingdom of God first but because they share their practical wisdom from a posture of vulnerability and transparency. Filled with penetrating questions and creative spiritual practices, *What Does Your Soul Love?* is an invitation to delve deep into the heart of our resistance and longings and discover the joy of keeping company with Jesus. I highly recommend it."

Sharon Garlough Brown, author of the Sensible Shoes series and *Shades of Light*

"Books on the subject of transformation abound. What makes this book stand out is that Gem and Alan crystallize for us what real change looks like through their very down-to-earth, living examples—concrete and relatable. One comes away after reading their accounts—peppered with story after story—convinced that authentic growth in God is indeed possible when our souls are focused in the right direction. Not only inspiring but downright practical!"

Wil Hernandez, executive director of CenterQuest, spiritual director, retreat leader, author

WHAT DOES YOUR SOUL LOVE?

EIGHT QUESTIONS THAT REVEAL GOD'S WORK IN YOU

GEM *and* ALAN FADLING

An imprint of InterVarsity Press
Downers Grove, Illinois

InterVarsity Press
P.O. Box 1400, Downers Grove, IL 60515-1426
ivpress.com
email@ivpress.com

InterVarsity Press® is the book-publishing division of InterVarsity Christian Fellowship/USA®, a
movement of students and faculty active on campus at hundreds of universities, colleges, and schools of
nursing in the United States of America, and a member movement of the International Fellowship of
Evangelical Students. For information about local and regional activities, visit intervarsity.org.

All Scripture quotations, unless otherwise indicated, are taken from The Holy Bible, New International
Version®, NIV®. Copyright © 1973, 1978, 1984, 2011 by Biblica, Inc.™ Used by permission of
Zondervan. All rights reserved worldwide. www.zondervan.com. The "NIV" and "New International
Version" are trademarks registered in the United States Patent and Trademark Office by Biblica, Inc.™

While any stories in this book are true, some names and identifying information may have been changed
to protect the privacy of individuals.

Cover design and image composite: David Fassett
Interior design: Jeanna Wiggins
Images: Circle ripples on water surface © Hiroshi Watanabe / Getty Images
        figure 1: Jeanna Wiggins © InterVarsity Press

ISBN 978-0-8308-4659-7 (print)
ISBN 978-0-8308-5820-0 (digital)

Printed in the United States of America ∞

InterVarsity Press is committed to ecological stewardship and to the conservation of natural resources in
all our operations. This book was printed using sustainably sourced paper.

Library of Congress Cataloging-in-Publication Data
A catalog record for this book is available from the Library of Congress.

P	20	19	18	17	16	15	14	13	12	11	10	9	8	7	6	5	4	3	2	1
Y	36	35	34	33	32	31	30	29	28	27	26	25	24	23	22	21	20	19

FROM GEM

*To Fred Harlan Wheat (1912–1990) and
Helen Violet Miller Wheat (1928–1995)*

Thank you, Mom, for being the first person to tell
me about God. You launched me into an incredible adventure.
Thank you, Dad, for blessing me with my name and for being the first
person to call out the mantle of leadership in my life.

FROM GEM AND ALAN

To Sean, Bryan, and Christopher

There are no words to describe how much we love each of you.
We could not be more proud of the men you have become.
May you learn early and deeply what it is your souls love.

CONTENTS

1

INVITATION

CHANGING FROM THE CENTER

THIS IS A BOOK ABOUT CHANGE. We set out to write a book about transformation, but in everyday life, the two of us have very different responses to change. Alan resists change, tending to avoid it. He prefers to keep things the way they are; he likes predictability as a way of feeling secure. Gem embraces change, even seeks it out. She loves the variety and creativity of new experiences. But we both are hungry for the kind of change God invites us to.

We seek the sort of transformation that would make us a little more beautiful in kingdom ways. We both want the kind of change that is an answer to "Your kingdom come, your will be done *in me* as it is in heaven."

SKIING OVER THE SURFACE

Alan grew up in Carmichael, California, a suburb of Sacramento, in a waterskiing family. If the weather allowed (and it usually did), you'd find his family at a nearby lake or on the Sacramento River waterskiing themselves to the point of exhaustion. Alan would often ski for an hour or more as his dad drove them up the river or back. He loved the magic of gliding across the surface of the water and not sinking like he would have if he was standing still.

But sometimes the sinking that happens when we're still is good, beautiful, and necessary. We're talking about the stillness and the sinking that need to happen when, for instance, we find ourselves skiing over the surface of our lives, when we let anxiety pull us along and we miss the depths, or when we get in a hurry and run past divine opportunities and appointments. If we would just stop occasionally and sink down, we'd get in touch with the deeper, more significant, even eternal, realities that we want to shape our lives. We'd get in touch with the immeasurable depths of love, peace, and joy that are available to us right now even as, racing along on the surface of our lives, we seek those somewhere out there.

And we are hardly the only ones to long for those depths. Quaker missionary and educator Thomas Kelly (1893–1941) wrote, "Deep within us all there is an amazing inner sanctuary of the soul, a holy place, a Divine Center, a speaking Voice, to which we may continually return." Kelly described this place as "the Shekinah of the soul, the Presence in the midst."[1] These depths are always with us. We are a kind of portable sanctuary, like the tabernacle that Israel carried along in their journey to the Promised Land (Numbers 1:50-51).

But too often, in the whirlwind of our thoughts and the rush of our activities, we skim along the surface of life and never experience these rich and life-giving depths. We don't tap into the reality of this Life—the One who is life who has come to make himself at home in our inner being. This idea is one that the apostle Paul returned to again and again. It seems to be the simplest way of communicating his understanding of the life of the gospel: Christ in us; Christ in me. This is a transforming friendship.

WILLING TO GIVE UP

Early in our marriage, Alan was a pastor to college students in a large Southern California church. We were both in our twenties, we didn't have kids, and I (Gem) had energy to spare. So in addition to working full time in the corporate world, I partnered with Alan in ministry. We so loved working with that group of students.

One day, a few days prior to our college group's upcoming missions trip to Mexico, I was getting ready for my day. Out of nowhere a question bubbled up: *If, while you are in Mexico, someone sees your camera and wants it, would you be willing to give it to them? Would you give up your camera?* I had a fancy and expensive Canon A-1 camera that shot film, so I spent some time pondering this question. After thinking a bit I decided that I could indeed give it up. I was aware that the people we were going to serve had limited resources, so it seemed best to me to be generous.

I continued preparing for the day ahead, and soon another thought emerged: *The camera is one thing, but would you be willing to give up Alan?* At this point, I was a bit stunned; what does this mean—give up Alan? I soon realized that I was being invited into a conversation with God. Just a few months prior, I had learned about and begun the practice of solitude and silence. I was learning how to listen to God in prayer and not just regale him with my monologue of requests. I knew I was in a dialogue at this point. I couldn't say a quick yes, because this was an extraordinarily serious question. It seemed to me to be an invitation to hold Alan loosely, to acknowledge that God was in charge of Alan's life.

I went into my home office to work and for four hours I wrestled with this question in between typing. A couple of times, as it arose, I answered, "I don't know."

Soon I was on a downhill slide into anxiety. I decided to call Alan at the church office to check in on him. In addition to his role as a pastor, he was in seminary at the time. He had a class that morning, but I thought he would have returned to his office by now. When he wasn't there, my worry increased. (This was back in the day of no cell phones and no "Find My Friends" app.)

The question returned: *Will you give up Alan?* Finally, I lifted my hands from my keyboard and decided to engage this question more fully. This may sound morbid and possibly melodramatic, but I let myself sink all the way down into the worst-case scenario of this question, just to try it on. I pictured in my mind what my life would be like without Alan. I let myself imagine it—a twenty-six-year-old widow. It was horrible, but I knew that I could carry on with my life and that God would be with me and would care for Alan. I took some deep breaths and decided that I could say, "Okay, I could give up Alan."

Fifteen minutes later, Alan called. Of course, I burst into tears and then explained to him, in detail, my entire morning—the question, the struggle, the resolution. He asked, "How long ago did you say that you answered yes?" I told him that it had been about fifteen minutes earlier. "Well," said Alan, "let me tell you what I was doing about fifteen minutes ago." He was on the freeway driving to church from seminary. Evidently the pace of both work and seminary had taken its toll. Alan momentarily fell asleep at the wheel. He woke up just in time to see that he was about to crash into a slow-moving dump truck. Fortunately, he swerved and made his way past with no harm.

We both imagined hearing the *Twilight Zone* theme and had a moment of being struck by the odd nature of the entire incident. I don't claim to understand exactly what was going on. I can't say if I hadn't said yes that Alan would have hit the truck; I don't think that's how God works. However, I believe God was asking me if I would dedicate Alan to God, let go of him and trust that God would care for him. God wanted Alan's life, in all ways possible, and God wanted me to trust him completely. I had just given Alan completely over to God to do whatever he wanted to do in his life. And, after having been married now for more than three decades, I'm still learning how that works.

This story is just one sample of the ways I have interacted with God on two levels at the same time over the course of my life. Getting ready for my work day, doing my job, *and* having a conversation about whether or not I will let go of my husband and consent to God doing his work in him. This simple awareness of a deeper level can develop into a lifetime of transformation.

A LIFE-GIVING AWARENESS

Most of us are aware of this inner soul dynamic at some level, but we may not process much of this awareness or, more importantly, talk about it with others. Yet this dynamic offers fuel for significant spiritual conversations that can grow us, refine us, and sharpen us. Paying attention to our soul helps us answer and discuss such questions as, "In what ways is God meeting me in my real everyday life?" and "What can I do to better see God, hear God, and walk with God?"

A passage of the spiritual classic *A Testament of Devotion* by Thomas R. Kelly offers a striking connection to the idea of a transforming life we are describing.

> "What can I do to better see God, hear God, and walk with God?"

There is a way of ordering our mental life on more than one level at once. On one level we may be thinking, discussing, seeing, calculating, meeting all the demands of external affairs. But deep within, behind the scenes, at a profounder level, we may also be in prayer and adoration, song and worship and a gentle receptiveness to divine breathings. . . . In a deeply religious culture people know that the deep level of prayer and of divine attendance is the most important thing in the world. It is at this deep level that the real business of life is determined. . . . Between the two levels is fruitful interplay, but ever the accent must be upon the deeper level, where the soul ever dwells in the presence of the Holy One.[2]

Kelly stirs a desire to be aware of those holy breathings, a longing to dip down into the inner dynamics of the soul. Pause and reread the text. Do you sense a continued invitation of the gentle receptiveness to divine breathings?

Embarking on a journey of transformation involves remaining awake to a deeper level of reality that is always present. Remaining on this journey requires a simpler, God focus. The eight questions posed in this book can help us cultivate this kind of deeper awareness and soul focus. They help keep us on the journey of transformation. They keep us in the presence of the transforming One.

IT'S ABOUT THE HEART

It will be very difficult to embark (and remain) on a journey of transformation if we do not have confidence that we are already loved as we currently are. We don't change so that we'll be loved more by God. We are measurelessly loved by God, so we are free and enabled to change in all the ways we long for.

When it comes to Jesus' strategy for changing the world, he began with a simple focus on the human heart. He did not set out primarily to change the way people behaved. He knew that without a change in the heart producing those behaviors, any outward change would be short-lived. Instead, he sought to help people see and embrace a vision of the kingdom of God on display in his life, his manner, his way. This was the model for the change to which he invited people.

> It will be very difficult to embark (and remain) on a journey of transformation if we do not have confidence that we are already loved as we currently are.

This was his message from the beginning: "Repent, for the kingdom of heaven has come near" (Matthew 3:2). *Repent* may not feel like a word of good news. To some ears, it sounds like "Stop everything you enjoy and become religious (and boring)." But Jesus was saying that change is good news, and that change is possible. You can go in a different direction—in the direction of the kingdom of heaven. Change is good news when it is change in the direction of alignment with the good, beautiful, and true purposes of God and his kingdom. Change is good news when it moves in the direction of fruitfulness that fulfills our deepest aspirations and blesses a world that needs it.

Jesus' message sounded so different from other Jewish preachers of his day. The Jewish leaders were far more interested and engaged in addressing behavior and even appearances. They wanted to be sure things looked right and that people behaved right (at least right as they defined it). They believed that they were doing the work of God, but they were remodeling the exteriors of an unchanged interior. Without a change of heart, outward change never lasts. Jesus was pursuing a strategy for transformation that would grow and last over decades, centuries, even millennia.

Though their own Scriptures said that God looks on the heart while humans focus on appearances, they still opted, maybe unconsciously, for an appearance-focused strategy. They polished the outside of the cup, as Jesus put it. They worked very hard to be seen by others as religiously impressive, and sought to hide anything in themselves that looked less than right.

> Without a change of heart, outward change never lasts.

A kingdom transformation approach brings what is ugly out into the open where it can be forgiven, cleansed, healed, transformed. Rather than avoiding fear, we lean into it and discover courage in the midst. Rather than numbing anxiety, we acknowledge its existence in God's presence. Facing reality is always better than avoiding it. An appearance management approach hides what is wrong, dirty, or broken so others won't see it. In this way, such realities grow more wrong, more broken. It takes layers of paint to whitewash those inner realities with an acceptable appearance.

Sometimes we opt for outward change as a substitute for the inward change to which God has been inviting us. In doing so we escape a change in soul by choosing a change of venue. But usually the change needed is in our soul, not our setting. We may be tempted to change churches, change jobs, or even change spouses because something doesn't feel right. Yet when we stop to discern, we may discover we are seeking a change "out there" to avoid a change "in here" that God may be leading us to welcome.

Transformation is also different from perfectionism. Perfectionism generally promotes pretending. Since none of us are perfect, we have to put on an appearance of perfection. But we are not writing this book from a place of having achieved perfection. We are still journeying in the valleys of transformation. We are all people in process who are sometimes more and sometimes less faithful to the journey.

We've noticed, however, that sometimes we are tempted to avoid necessary change because the pain of what's unwell seems easier to endure that the unknown pain we imagine in the path of change. We must learn to cultivate awareness around our resistance to change as a surface reaction to a deeper and better invitation.

It can help to remember that we are not the prime movers in this transformation. The language of transformation in the New Testament, for example, is in the passive voice. Rather than being initiators of the action, we are responders to the action of another. We are being transformed rather than transforming ourselves. There is a divine work with which we cooperate. The work of cooperating is critical, but not primary. The transforming work of God through the potent action of God's Spirit is what is primary.

Think about the familiar language in the book of Romans:

> Therefore, I urge you, brothers and sisters, in view of God's mercy, to offer your bodies as a living sacrifice, holy and pleasing to God—this is your true and proper worship. Do not conform to the pattern of this world, *but be transformed by the renewing of your mind.* Then you will be able to test and approve what God's will is—his good, pleasing and perfect will. (Romans 12:1-2, emphasis added)

In the light of our growing confidence in the ever-present mercy of God, we seek to offer our whole selves to abide in the holy, joyful, and transforming presence of God. Doing this is a worship-centric way to live and bears the fruit of reorienting us away from the life-draining patterns of this world and transforming us into the pattern of God's good, pleasing, and perfect intentions for us. In this we are positioned to shine in the world in a way that just might recommend the kingdom of God to others living life with us. We learn to see reality through the eyes of Jesus.

Elsewhere, Paul reminds us that "the Lord is the Spirit, and where the Spirit of the Lord is, there is freedom. And we all, who with unveiled faces contemplate the Lord's glory, *are being transformed into his image* with ever-increasing glory, which comes from the Lord, who is the Spirit" (2 Corinthians 3:17-18, emphasis added). As the Spirit opens our eyes to see God's beauty more clearly, we increasingly reflect the image of God to those around us. Contemplating glory is a transforming invitation God extends to anyone who will respond.

So, transformation is not something we seek directly. It is the "all these things will be given to you as well" (Matthew 6:33) that comes in the wake of seeking God first, aligning ourselves with divine reality, and walking in the truth. Transformation is the fruit of cooperating with and responding to divine activity.

All of this talk of transformation presupposes malformation. We aren't all that God has intended us to be. Sin is more than just immorality. It is turning our vocations upsidedown to become self-serving rather than living our lives for the good of others. We choose idolatry over ministry. We have habits of thought and behavior that distance us from God rather than

draw us near. Through any number of forces, we've been mal-
formed. But this is not final. We are invited to the reordering of
our disordered desires. As we let the desires of the Spirit reorder
the false desires of our without-God selves, we can be transformed in friendship with God.

The eight questions we suggest in this book are not the only
ones that exist for transformation. There are a multitude of ways
God might work within us the transformation he intends. These
questions simply represent key insights we've discovered and re-
visited often in our own journeys of transformation, which have
led to an energizing, encouraging, joyful, and ever-changing life.

There have been many times when our lives felt more like a
series of disconnected events than a continual path. But when
we see our lives primarily as separate and unrelated events, we
miss the journey of transformation implicit in our moments and
days. Transformation happens over time—like taking a journey
or walking a path. Each step relates to those that have gone
before and those that lie ahead. Transformation is a process.

This journey is an opportunity to become skilled at living in
the reality of the kingdom. It is a process of coming to live with
more practiced facility in the ways the kingdom works here on
earth. This is the direction of our transformation. We move from
learning, talking, or thinking about those ways to experimenting
with and eventually embodying them. We grow humbly confident in the ways of interactive friendship with Jesus our Master.

The transforming invitation of Jesus is the same one Jesus
extended to his first followers: an invitation to be a student, an
apprentice, a disciple. It's unfortunate that sometimes the word
discipleship has come to feel cliché and almost empty of meaning.
We should experience discipleship to Jesus as the great honor

that it is: being personally mentored by the master of life himself. It could be an apprenticeship of joy, hope, peace, and a fruitfulness beyond imagining.

This transforming process with Jesus is relational and interactive. It is progressive. It is real-life and authentic. It is Spirit-guided and Spirit-empowered. It leads us into and through the best life available to us: the life of the kingdom.

ASKING GREAT QUESTIONS

As a spiritual director and a formation practitioner, Gem is always on the lookout for great questions. Right up there next to learning to listen well, learning to ask great questions is crucial to walking alongside others. Gem has learned more about asking questions through a small group of gifted women who get together twice a year. The group is a place to share lives, engage in creative spiritual practices, and pray for one another. It is a soul-filling time. One of the women in the group is Jane Willard, a treasured mentor, friend, and consistent reservoir of wisdom.

Typically, when someone shares their latest musings, longings, or fears, Jane will pop in at the end with a short, simple question. And it is always dead on. Her question goes right to the heart of what was shared, unravels it (in a good way), and gives a way forward that feels life giving. It's a true gift. She doesn't tell anyone what to do. She simply asks a question that lays a path to walk on.

As we've prepared to write this book together, we've taken the time to think back over the last many years of our own spiritual journeys. We've asked ourselves: What questions have helped us to take next steps in our lives with God? What insights have caused us to dig deeper into our own inner work?

Eight questions rose to the surface and became the frame for this book. It is not an exhaustive list, but a personal one. Like Jane, we want to be people who ask wisdom-filled, life-giving, gracious questions. Insights to those questions will arise in conversation with our loving God. Our hope is that these questions will spur you on to your next movement forward in transformation.

We have written this book together—in deep conversation and dialogue. The ideas move back and forth between us as we both wrote in each chapter. Much of the book has a unified voice without distinction between us. However, where we told specific personal stories we have indicated the speaker in the text as we did in this chapter.

> We move at the pace of grace. We grow at the pace of transformation.

You'll also find a number of resources along the way that we hope will help you sink deeper into these eight questions:

- *Process words.* Cultivating an orientation to transformation often involves learning a new vocabulary. Throughout the book, Gem has gathered, defined, and described a number of words that help us remain open to all of the fullness that God has to offer on our journey of transformation. Some words act as brake pedals and others act as accelerators. The language we use either hinders or helps transformation both for ourselves and for others. These process words have encouraged continued change in our lives and we hope they help you move forward as well.

- *Exercises.* You'll find a few exercises in the course of the book. Jesus reminds us that when we know something, we'll actually be blessed when we take action (see John

13:17). While it may be tempting to do them later, we encourage you as you read to take breaks to try these exercises on. They've been helpful to us.

- *Reflection questions.* At the end of each chapter you'll find a set of questions that may be useful for personal reflection and journaling as well as for group discussion. These questions will be particularly helpful as you engage Appendix C: Guide for Groups.

Remember, we move at the pace of grace. We grow at the pace of transformation. You have all the time you need in God's loving care. The invitation here is to let God show you how he wants to meet you and walk with you personally on your life's journey.

BE TRANSFORMED

Busyness

1. We can't miss the day-to-day level of life, but what keeps you less aware of the deeper level of your life?

2. What are some possibilities for growing your awareness of the connection between the inner and the outer levels of your life?

3. What are you doing to attend to your soul, to that deepest level of who you are? *Time to reflect, Tuesday*

4. In prayer, ask God to help you engage in the fruitful interplay of your soul life and your day-to-day life.

2

DESIRE

WHAT DO YOU REALLY WANT?

Slow—*It's okay for things to take time. We can be efficient and productive in our outer life, but our souls can only go so fast. In North America, slow is a countercultural word. There is nothing good about slow in the eyes of this fast-moving, go-go-go culture. Yet our soul can only move as fast as the speed of transformation. Transformation takes time. So it is good to accept that and allow the inner pace of our lives to move at that speed.*

A FEW TIMES A MONTH you can find us walking the bluffs of a nearby beach town. The lulling sound of the waves is a rhythm that our souls deeply love, and we find that we naturally slow to a stroll on these days. Simply being near the water with all of its sights, sounds, and smells grants us effortless delight.

We gaze at the surface, but what lies below the depths, the parts hidden from eye's view? Today we have documentaries that reveal the various parts of the ocean. But there was a time when humans hadn't yet found ways of documenting what was underneath the surface of the sea. In fact, little was known about the oceans until the late 1800s. Stories and myths had given us imagined creatures that hid in the depths of the sea, but most scientists thought the deep sea was uninhabitable because of the cold and dark. Even Socrates, the Greek philosopher, said, "Everything is corroded by the brine, and there is no vegetation worth mentioning, and scarcely any degree of perfect formation, but only caverns and sand and measureless mud, and tracts of slime."[1]

Years later, in a book published in 1859, Edward Forbes wrote, "As we descend deeper and deeper in this region, its inhabitants become more and more modified, and fewer and fewer, indicating our approach towards an abyss where life is either extinguished, or exhibits but a few sparks to mark its lingering presence."[2]

However, just a few years later, in 1864, father and son naturalists Michael and Georg Ossian Sars were the first to bring sea lilies to shore from 10,000 feet beneath the surface. Sea lilies are beautiful creatures that look like a cross between a delicate spider and a flower with featherlike arms. Of course, the scientific community was thrilled to learn that the deep was apparently inhabited. Many years later, Georg Sars wrote, "So far was I from observing any sign of diminished intensity in this animal life at increased depths, that it seemed, on the contrary, as if there was just beginning to appear a rich and, in many respects, peculiar deep-sea Fauna, of which only a very incomplete notion had previously existed."[3]

Like the sea lily, our desires can sometimes hide, deep down inside of us. Desire can be a beautiful, delicate creature that we are unaware of unless we go on a relentless search of our inner depths. Like the scientists and great thinkers of the past, we may not believe that there is anything deep inside of us. We see no evidence of our desires at the higher depths and so we don't go exploring.

The bottom of the ocean is hidden to most of us but, as we've discovered, it contains beauty and life. Just as God created the ocean and everything in its depths, he sees and knows those deep places within us, even if we don't see or know what's happening there. What would it be like for you to go on your own spiritual submersible exploration to glimpse what is in your deepest levels of desire?

The ocean of God's love is enormous.

You may not have the ability right now to see, discern, or enjoy what lies in those depths. However, as you are ready, God may give you the vision to see what is there, what he has created, what he has been nurturing. There are aspects of you that, although hidden, are no less beautiful or valuable.

As you dive into the deep level of desire, let this add to your understanding of how much God loves you. The ocean of God's love is enormous. It is good to feel the grandness of that at times, as it can give a sense of freedom. God's love is greater than you can imagine.

The creatures in the ocean depths remind us that there is unfathomable beauty in the deepest and darkest of places. Sometimes it is fear that keeps us from looking deeper. We are afraid we will find something unknown or even ugly. But it is in this deeper level that we also find hidden beauty. Stay open, and let God show you in his time and in his way.

WHAT DO I REALLY WANT?

Let's begin with a relatively benign search for a deeper desire. I (Gem) am talking about my *wants* here. *What I want* lives on various levels. For example, I *want* to eat whatever I want, whenever I want. That has been a lifelong, unspoken desire. And, for the most part, I have been able to do just that without much consequence. I've had a great metabolism and have been able to maintain a relatively heathy existence. Until I reached my mid-forties. Then everything came to a screeching halt. My metabolism slowed and my ability to digest processed foods diminished. What I wanted was to keep everything the way it was. But for the sake of my health, I've had to go down into the depths on a search for a deeper desire, the desire for good health. What I most deeply want is to be healthy and to live a long, full life.

However, many years later I still battle this deeper desire for long-term health. I let my surface desire for a sensation of fullness and my inclination toward unhealthy foods rule the day. I am in touch with my deepest desire, but I am not yet living fully from that place. This is a work in progress for me, and sometimes I get discouraged by how long it is taking. I know others who have the ability to flip a switch and simply decide what they will and won't eat. I apparently don't have that switch.

But here's the thing: I have not yet given up. I haven't stopped seeking to make food decisions based on my deeper desire for long-term health. The real issue for me is deeper than just the food. I know the reason this is taking so long is that I am a comfort eater, as food can mask anxiety and a number of other issues. It's about my inner hunger for satisfaction and fullness. Meeting myself at this level means acknowledging my depths and requires getting in touch with my truest desires. So I won't give up. I trust that God will meet me in this deep place of yearning for fullness and satisfaction. I'm determined to keep responding to invitations until I make my way to living from my truest, deepest self. At some point, I will be free enough not to let my taste buds be the boss of me.

Now let's take a look at someone whose desire erupted out of sheer desperation. Sometimes you don't have to go searching for desire. It emerges because you have no other choice, and it forces you to action.

In Luke 8 we learn about a woman who had suffered with bleeding for twelve years. Twelve years is a long time. In that day, she would have been considered unclean, which meant she not only physically suffered but was also socially ostracized. Jesus was passing by, making his way to heal the daughter of a synagogue leader. The crowds were following Jesus and pressing in from all sides.

The level of desire within this woman for healing was strong and pulled her toward Jesus like a magnet to iron. She must have been scared to death, so much so that she turned this into a covert operation. Someone in her condition could not be near, let alone touch, a rabbi. If only she could touch the hem of Jesus' cloak. Her desire for healing overcame her great fear. Jesus and the disciples were making their way through a pushing and shoving crowd. Sandals, feet, and dust were everywhere. And this woman, trying desperately to be unseen, reached out a finger toward the hem of Jesus' cloak amidst the dusty sandals. Hoping against hope for a miracle. Her desire propelled her to act. And Jesus responded. "Who touched me?" (Luke 8:45). The disciples thought he was crazy because of the crushing crowd. But Jesus wanted more for this woman, more than a stolen healing touch. Fearfully, she came forward.

What followed were a few simple sentences of love: "Daughter, your faith has healed you. Go in peace" (Luke 8:48). Jesus took the time to stop even though he was on his way to help a dying girl. This woman mattered to him. He not only healed her, he gave her time, attention, and value. He met her at levels of desire she probably didn't even know existed.

By calling her daughter, he showed a relationship of love. By letting her know that her faith made her well, he gave her dignity and respect. By sharing peace, he gave her his blessing. By ending her suffering, he showed that he was all powerful and able to heal. The encounter is a beautiful example of healing and making someone clean and whole.

EXERCISE

This woman's desire, desperation, and her belief in who Jesus was caused her to overcome all of her barriers and reach out.

Would you like to come to Jesus in this same way?

In what area of your life do you need the deepest healing?

In what area of your life do you feel the most unclean?

Is there an aspect of yourself that makes you want to hide?

What would it take for you to step forward in faith, to reach to Jesus for help or healing?

Let the depth of your desire for wholeness propel you forward. And when you are ready, reach out.

A MATTER OF FOCUS

The relationship between desire and transformation is the matter of focus. David offers a powerful statement of focus in Psalm 27:

One thing I ask from the LORD,
    this only do I seek:
that I may dwell in the house of the LORD
    all the days of my life,
to gaze on the beauty of the LORD
    and to seek him in his temple. (Psalm 27:4)

In David's prayerful communion with God, he tells us that there is only one thing he asks, only one thing he seeks. Then, he describes three facets of this singular search: He wants to dwell in the Lord's house every day of his life. He wants to gaze on the beauty of the Lord. He wants to seek the Lord in his temple. The focus of David's desires is God. David's "one thing" was to be at home with God, to continually contemplate the beauty of God, and to honor God through the worship of his words and his life.

When we are in a hurry, our desires seem to spin out of control. Hurry creates a centrifugal dynamic that can pull us away from the vital center David seeks. Hurry can cause us to feel as though we don't have a home, a safe, stable, secure place to stand. But the Lord invites us to be at home *in* him. In a world that feels so gaudy, garish, and brash in its depiction of what's attractive, we're grateful for the simple invitation to gaze on the Lord's eternal beauty. At a time when the holy seems the last thing on our culture's mind, we are invited to seek the Lord in his temple.

Signs of this simple, central focus of desire are expressed in a number of other biblical stories. For example, hear it in the interaction of Jesus, Martha, and Mary. Remember these lines? "'Martha, Martha,' the Lord answered, 'you are worried and upset about many things, but few things are needed—or indeed only one. Mary has chosen what is better, and it will not be taken away from her'" (Luke 10:41-42).

Understandably, Martha, the hostess, was distracted and concerned about many details. Martha wanted to be a good host. Martha wanted to serve Jesus well. Martha wanted many things. But Jesus wanted her to realize what matters most and to keep her focus on that. So Jesus speaks a singular invitation to Martha, which Mary has already responded to. Jesus affirms Mary's choice of activity and heart focus: Mary had understood what one thing is necessary in this life. What is it?

"Mary . . . sat at the Lord's feet listening to what he said" (Luke 10:39). Mary's sole focus was Jesus—listening to Jesus, being with Jesus, being a friend of Jesus, and being a student of Jesus. That focus is a wise choice because we have much to learn from him. Jesus, for instance, is an absolute genius when it comes to living the fullest and best possible life. Jesus knows how to help us live into the fullness of our God-given desires.

Just as David focused on the Lord God, Mary focused on Jesus. She wanted to spend time with him and to learn from him. She chose to be with him and give him her undivided attention whenever she could. As his student, she was taking the path of transformation.

When it comes to the focus of our desire, think of Paul the apostle.

Not that I have already obtained all this, or have already arrived at my goal, but I press on to take hold of that for which Christ Jesus took hold of me. Brothers and sisters, I do not consider myself yet to have taken hold of it. But one thing I do: Forgetting what is behind and straining toward what is ahead, I press on toward the goal to win the prize for which God has called me heavenward in Christ Jesus. (Philippians 3:12-14)

Paul was pressing on to take hold of his "one thing" that he hadn't yet fully grasped. We can also seek to forget the past and strain forward to what lies ahead. We can pursue the prize to which God has called us. But what is this "one thing"? "Whatever were gains to me I now consider loss for the sake of Christ. What is more, I consider everything a loss because of *the surpassing worth of knowing Christ Jesus my Lord*, for whose sake I have lost all things" (Philippians 3:7-8, emphasis added).

In his past, there were many things Paul wanted. He wanted to excel beyond any of his peers in the Pharisee way of life. He wanted to oppose, even attack, anyone associated with the misguided and blasphemous Jesus movement. He wanted to be blameless in his keeping of the law of God (Philippians 3:5-6). But now, having encountered this Jesus he once opposed, he's come to realize "the surpassing worth of knowing Christ Jesus my Lord." Paul's past desires for religious achievements, a favored pedigree, and an impeccable heritage have ceased to be appealing. They were not a path of transformation. Instead, he has come to focus all of his desire on the immeasurable value of being in a transforming relationship with Jesus.

Transformation does this in us. A simple focus on following Jesus has a way, over time, of drawing in all of our other desires until they are woven into a unifying desire for Jesus himself. What we once treasured and sought with passion fades in value next to the treasure of knowing Jesus. We might even come to see our past passions as distractions, even losses, by comparison.

In another encounter, Jesus speaks with compassion to the wealthy young man seeking counsel from him. The man asked, "What must I do to inherit eternal life?" (Mark 10:17). It's a strategic question. And how did Jesus respond? "Jesus looked at him and loved him. 'One thing you lack,' he said. 'Go, sell everything you have and give to the poor, and you will have treasure in heaven. Then come, follow me'" (Mark 10:21).

Jesus sees the man and his heart goes out to him. Perhaps we in the West would be surprised at such compassion. It would seem that the wealthy should be the ones offering charity. But Jesus really sees him. He issues a "one thing" invitation to him. He sees that this man is caught by, perhaps even trapped in, his own wealth.

The "one thing" this man lacked was not material. What he lacked was a life-giving focus on the One who is life. When he heard Jesus' answer, "the man's face fell. He went away sad, because he had great wealth" (Mark 10:22). His many possessions were the focus of his desires, and they were keeping him from experiencing the reality of eternal living that Jesus was offering. He couldn't let go of that to which he clung. Jesus knows this about each of us. He may invite us to give up something, but he does this so that our hands might be open and ready to receive God's priceless gift of lasting life.

Maybe we're not that different from this wealthy man. It can be tempting to define our "one thing" only in terms of the work we do. (This is the way in which we gain wealth anyway.) That's helpful as far as it goes, but we've come to believe that the focus of our work is rooted in the focus of our lives.

Put differently, what we do in our work is meant to be like a satellite orbiting the sun of our one main thing of knowing Jesus, being a friend of Jesus, being at home with Jesus, orienting the whole of our lives around Jesus. If we want to live our lives and do our work in a way that glorifies God, then letting Jesus be the growing focus of our whole heart's desire becomes our "one thing." Thinking in "one thing" terms focuses our lives and therefore simplifies our work.

> **Thinking in "one thing" terms focuses our lives and therefore simplifies our work.**

Now, all of this does not negate the very real desires in our hearts. There is much God has given us to want. Notice this beautiful prayer David prays for his friends.

> May he give you the desire of your heart
> and make all your plans succeed.
> May we shout for joy over your victory
> and lift up our banners in the name of our God.
> May the LORD grant all your requests. (Psalm 20:4-5)

We are grateful for these words, both as a personal prayer that others might offer and as a way to pray for our friends. It's important that David prays God would give them "the desire of your heart." Note that *desire* is singular here, not plural. We're back in "one thing" territory. David wants them to know and experience the fulfilling of their deepest desire, the desire *of their hearts*. And their deepest, truest desire is to want God, to love God.

The desire of our heart is in a different category than the desires of the culture around us, the desires that advertisers seek to breed, or the desires for something out there we think will satisfy us. We were made to desire, but desire gets hijacked or distorted in so many ways. Our God-given desire to enjoy the gift of good food gets hijacked and becomes gluttony. Our

God-given desire to love and be loved gets bent into lust. Our
holy desire to enjoy good things from God gets commandeered
and becomes greed. And so it can be with any of our God-given
desires. On the path of transformation, God graciously and
firmly seeks to awaken us to ways in which our desires have
been misdirected. He exposes distorted desires that masquerade
as what we truly want. They pretend to be real and substantial
when they are really illusory and hollow.

Like Gem, my (Alan) desires as they relate to food are a continuing place of transformation for me. Sometimes it feels like
these desires are the most resistant to change. When John
Cassian was cataloguing some of the ways that desire gets hijacked in his fourth-century writings, the first distorted desire
he dealt with was the one focused on food: gluttony. The need
to eat is a basic reality of our lives. We might be able to go hours
without food on a normal day, or we may intentionally fast for a
number of days, but food is a significant part of our normal,
everyday life. We must eat to live even though we don't live only
by the food we eat (Matthew 4:4). We can welcome the gift of
good food and eat it with freedom and gratitude, or we can seek
some sort of soul fulfillment in the filling of our bellies. The first
is a gift. The second is a trap.

When it comes to my ongoing relationship to food, I find
myself asking questions like, *What if I really don't live by bread
alone? What if I have nourishment that is greater than the food I put
in my mouth? What do I really want as it relates to food: to lose
weight or to live healthy and whole as it relates to the gift of food?
Do I believe there is a way of eating well that is truly satisfying?*

I sometimes imagine my disordered desires for food like they
are whiny children or temperamental teens. They want what

they want when they want it. When I eat in keeping with my disordered desires for food, I don't feel well. I begin to be burdened, literally, by my choices. I imagine these juvenile desires being present when I'm eating unhealthy food or too much food but being conveniently absent when it comes time to experience the consequences of those choices. Disordered desire is there for the pleasure but abandons me in the aftermath.

This is why I am still learning how to bring my desires for food into relationship with my generous Provider. I do not eat apart from God, but with God. I need to learn to discern my food impulses, the "feel likes" and the cravings that arise within me. They are not all good. I don't do well to mindlessly follow them. They do not all lead to life.

This "one thing" focus also comes into play in our work. A lot of my work is focused on writing and speaking at retreats and in consultation and conference settings. When we think of highly visible companies, many of them have a singular focus. Apple makes insanely great personal technologies. In-N-Out makes delicious hamburgers. Starbucks aims at great coffee. These are great examples of an organizational focus.

I'm coming to find that my singular focus on following Jesus has a way of focusing my vocational life as well. However, though I seek to have this sort of "one thing" focus in my life and my work, I am still human and, too often, weak. Sometimes I live an anxious, distracted life and find myself bouncing back and forth between my many concerns, many responsibilities, many relationships, many opportunities, and many priorities. And when my life is about dozens of things that I'm trying to manage well, I become overwhelmed.

But when I remember that my life revolves around a single hub, then I see every concern, responsibility, relationship, opportunity, and priority in my life as a spoke finding its focus at that hub. This simpler—biblical and therefore much improved—perspective changes the attitude of my heart and my mind. Then I am able to live with peace rather than anxiety, focus rather than distraction, and rootedness rather than volatility. This "one thing" reality— Jesus—becomes a unifying center for all the many things in my day-to-day life. Drawing close to Jesus, abiding in Jesus, walking with Jesus, enjoying Jesus, and bearing the good fruit of friendship with Jesus keep me from being overwhelmed by all the spokes. There is simply the next step to take in my work—a step I take with Jesus just ahead of me.

> This "one thing" reality——Jesus——becomes a unifying center for all the many things in my day-to-day life.

The "one thing" focus is not limiting or reductionist; rather, it is focused and rich. When Paul wrote his letter to his friends in Colossi, he had a lot to say about fullness of life. For example, he tells them that he had become a servant to the people of God in order to be able to present God's Word in all its fullness (Colossians 1:25). What is this fullness? What is the profound richness of what God has to say to us through his Son Jesus? Paul referred to it as a mystery and as "glorious riches" that had been hidden for ages and ages, for generation after generation, but had now been uncovered and disclosed to God's people (Colossians 1:26-27). What was this mystery? What had God's people come to understand? What message is so rich, so glorious, so significant that Paul wanted us all to know it? Simply put, it is "Christ in you, the hope of glory" (Colossians 1:27).

This is the transforming desire we are invited to. This is the rich reality that lies at the center of our lives. Christ in us as his people provides context and purpose for everything we do. Christ in our hearts. Christ in our bodies. Christ in our community. The living Christ actually with us. What more could we want?

MAKING REQUESTS

Transformation can sometimes get stuck in the land of *have tos, shoulds,* and *oughts.* What is your deepest, God-given desire and in what ways has that desire been distorted? Holy desire can get pushed down or forgotten. We can give ourselves space to lay down our own expectations (and those of others) to get in touch with what we truly and deeply *want.* Desire can flourish in this environment. This kind of grace empowers transformation.

> What is your deepest, God-given desire, and in what ways has that desire been distorted?

Do you ever find yourself wondering about the necessity of making requests in prayer? God already knows what we are going to say, right? He already knows what he is going to do. This may, at times, cause making requests to seem pointless. St. Augustine discusses this in his *Letter to Proba*:

> Why God should ask us to pray, when he knows what we need before we ask him, may perplex us if we do not realize that our Lord and God does not want to know what we want (for he cannot fail to know it) but wants us rather to exercise our desire through our prayers, so that we may be able to receive what he is preparing to give us. His gift is very great indeed, but our capacity is too small and limited to receive it.[4]

Augustine points out our limited thinking and then offers a viable way forward. We can discover and share our desires through our prayers. We can be enlarged so that we are able to receive what God is preparing to give (no matter what that may be). Getting in touch with our desires, sharing them with God, and growing through that is all a part of our transformational process.

WHAT WOULD JESUS DESIRE?

Most of us remember the craze from quite a few years back. Bumper stickers and bracelets all emblazoned with four simple initials: WWJD? (What Would Jesus Do?). We'd like to suggest another word for the *D* in WWJD: What Would Jesus *Desire*? What does Jesus want for you? We can seek to discern what is on the heart of Jesus as he seeks to transform us from the inside out. It is possible to continue to reach down into our own depths and learn to cooperate with his desires.

The story of the friends who lowered the man into the presence of Jesus from the roof above gives us a peek into a way we might place ourselves before Jesus.

One day Jesus was teaching, and Pharisees and teachers of the law were sitting there. They had come from every village of Galilee and from Judea and Jerusalem. And the power of the Lord was with Jesus to heal the sick. Some men came carrying a paralyzed man on a mat and tried to take him into the house to lay him before Jesus. When they could not find a way to do this because of the crowd, they went up on the roof and lowered him on his mat through the tiles into the middle of the crowd, right in front of Jesus.

When Jesus saw their faith, he said, "Friend, your sins are forgiven." The Pharisees and the teachers of the law began thinking to themselves, "Who is this fellow who speaks blasphemy? Who can forgive sins but God alone?" Jesus knew what they were thinking and asked, "Why are you thinking these things in your hearts? Which is easier: to say, 'Your sins are forgiven,' or to say, 'Get up and walk'? But I want you to know that the Son of Man has authority on earth to forgive sins." So he said to the paralyzed man, "I tell you, get up, take your mat and go home." Immediately he stood up in front of them, took what he had been lying on and went home praising God. Everyone was amazed and gave praise to God. They were filled with awe and said, "We have seen remarkable things today." (Luke 5:17-26)

This level of friendship is hard to come by. These men were willing to bring harm to property, disrupt a meeting, and make fools of themselves just so they could get their friend into the presence of Jesus.

Neither the friends nor the paralyzed man ever made a request. They simply lowered their friend down, and Jesus immediately responded to this act of faith. He knew, on every level, what the paralyzed man wanted. He dealt with his soul first ("Your sins are forgiven"). Then he brought healing to his body ("Get up, take your mat and go home").

We can be our own "set of friends" as we let our desire for transformation and healing meet up with Jesus' desire to transform and to heal. He already knows what we need, even more than we do. We can linger in his presence so that he may do what he most deeply desires to do in our lives. What might that look like?

EXERCISE

Imagine yourself in this scene. You are the person on the mat. Your friends have broken through the roof and are now lowering you down into the room. Your fear is completely overshadowed by the fact that you believe Jesus has the power to help you. So you stay on the mat as you come closer and closer to the floor right in front of Jesus. You know who he is. You've heard him teach. You've seen him heal. Jesus is loving, and his authority is unmatched.

What enters your mind as you see Jesus' face?

What would Jesus most desire for you right now?

What might he say?

Linger here in trust for a moment. Your intention is that Jesus would do what he wants most for you. Let your agenda drop and let his desire raise to the surface.

Thank Jesus for embracing you. Thank him for extending his grace to you.

Let yourself fill with awe at his love, care, and ability.

Like the sea lily, your desires may be hidden in your depths. Let it become the symbol of your desire to discover something under the surface. Be willing to go exploring. Find out what you truly desire underneath the surface of your circumstances. And learn, by listening in prayer, to become aware of what Jesus himself might desire for you. Let God guide you into undiscovered depths by his grace.

BE TRANSFORMED

1. Consider an area of your life in which you have been stuck in the shallows. Take a few moments to get into your inner

depths, and see if you can locate some deeper desires. What do you see?

2. What is one way you can bring greater focus to your desires?

3. What is your "one thing"?

4. Take some time imagining yourself in the presence of Jesus, just like the paralytic. What might Jesus desire for you right now? Linger here.

3

RESISTANCE

WHAT IS GETTING IN YOUR WAY?

Seasons—*There is a time for everything (Ecclesiastes 3:1-8). A person's life is full of many different seasons. Single, married, children, empty nest, workplace, mid-life. Not to mention the seasons of your soul. Let yourself be in the season you are in, and mine it for all it's worth. Give yourself grace in winter. Remember that roots are going deep and sap is replenishing. Rejoice in the beauty of spring. Revel in the new beginnings. Bask in the sun of summer. Relish the time for play and recreation. Give thanks in the abundance of fall. Enjoy bringing in the harvest.*

And—*Ahhhh. Take a deep breath on that one. It can nicely replace* but. *"Well, that's all well and good, but . . ." But shuts the conversation down and negates what came before it. And opens up for further ideas and discussion. But is a conversation killer because you know that whatever came before it is being negated and what*

comes after the but is how it really is. We can easily see how this might
work in relationship. It is wonderful in keeping the communication
flowing. It is true that most of us want to be heard and understood,
and we often don't realize that we can give ourselves those gifts.
And keeps you validated and heard within yourself. Find ways to
replace but with and. See what happens to you in terms of optimism
and hope.

C YCLING IS A DELIGHT, especially in Southern California, where most days the weather cooperates. I (Alan) love long rides of an hour or more. But right alongside my good intentions, I also find within myself resistance that sounds something like, *I feel too tired to cycle today, It's too hot (or too cold) to cycle today,* or *I'll probably feel more like cycling tomorrow.* I imagine that getting dressed for cycling will be too much of a hassle.

These resistances rarely feel like a shout. They usually sound more like an insistent whisper within that leans against the good that I intend. I need to remember that what I don't feel like in the moment is often something I deeply and truly desire, and what I feel like is often something my true self rejects. My surface impulses and my deep desires are not the same.

It's as though my inner resistance presents itself as a brick wall. And I can't walk through brick walls. I might be able to make my way through with the help of a sledgehammer, but, left to myself, a brick wall is an insurmountable barrier. But what I discover when I lean into my thoughts and feelings of resistance to the good that lies before me is that resistance is more like tissue paper painted to *look* like a brick wall. I lean on it, expecting great resistance, and discover the very act of pushing in exposes that my resistance is as thin as tissue paper.

So, when I lean in to my resistance, getting on my bicycle in spite of it, within moments I find that I'm glad to be out and riding. I feel grateful and alive having acted on the good I intended. My resistance turned out to be wrong. This is important. For me, it's a matter of faith. What do I believe to be true, God-given impulses within me?

Henri Nouwen described his own resistance to the creative work he felt called to do:

> It is remarkable how hard it is to sit down quietly and trust our own creativity. There seems to be a deep-seated resistance to writing. I have experienced this resistance myself over and over again. Even after many years of writing, I experience real fear when I face the empty page. Why am I so afraid? Sometimes I have an imaginary reader in mind who is looking over my shoulder and rejecting every word I write down. Sometimes I am overwhelmed by the countless books and articles that already have been written and I cannot imagine that I have anything to say that hasn't already been said better by someone else. Sometimes it seems that every sentence fails to express what I really want to say and that written words simply cannot hold what goes on in my mind and heart. These fears sometimes paralyze me and make me delay or even abandon my writing plans.[1]

Me too. Resistance such as fears or worries that bubble up in my emotions or thoughts haven't gone away as I engage my own work. I've had a version of every thought Nouwen mentioned above. You probably have too in your own work.

So, the resistance we are talking about here is a resistance to what is good, beautiful, and true that rises up from within us. It isn't an outwardly focused resistance or an other-provoked resistance. It is our own "I don't feel like it," or "That worries me," or "I'm afraid" rising up within. *Resistance* here is a word for the impulses that rise up within us against the good invitation to live a more transformed life.

These thoughts and feelings of resistance often seem quite substantial. If they didn't, we probably wouldn't give them much attention. But, in the spirit of Augustine's idea of evil as an absence of good (rather than something substantial in itself), resistance really doesn't have substance. These impulses are a negative. They are an absence of something rather than the presence of something. Our depressed or despairing mood is an absence of joy

> Resistance is the opposite of sinking our roots deep into an abiding friendship with a real and present God.

and hope (which are actually tangible fruit of the presence of God with us). When we believe our inner resistances to be real and substantial, it's almost as though we become a ghost because of our strong belief in something that isn't.

In that sense, resistance is the opposite of sinking our roots deep into an abiding friendship with a real and present God. It is the opposite of resting and lingering with God. It is letting impulses that would distance us from God win the day. It is our arms pushing against God instead of welcoming and embracing God. It is our eyes looking elsewhere rather than gazing upon God. It is our hearts wandering rather than being set on things above. Transformation stalls when resistance steers our steps.

LIVING IN THE KINGDOM

Some of us have grown up in a context where we were taught that the body and the Pauline concept of flesh were the same thing.

This kind of "body is bad" theology doesn't help us do things God is inviting us to do, like honor him with our bodies (1 Corinthians 6:20). How could we honor God with something bad?

The flesh here is not the physical body, but a way of life we've grown used to living in a world that does not recognize the reality of God and his kingdom. It is a dynamic within whereby we grab for what we need, not trusting (or knowing of) God's generosity to provide what we need. It is an "I can do it myself" approach to living that presumes the absence of a loving God.

Our bodies, however, are God-given gifts to us. The ways that we sometimes use our bodies isn't. We can do godless things that reinforce unholy, destructive habits and patterns in our bodies. But our bodies themselves are good.

A few passages from Paul's letter to the Galatians offer help in addressing resistance. For example, "I have been crucified with Christ and I no longer live, but Christ lives in me. The life I now live in the body, I live by faith in the Son of God, who loved me and gave himself for me" (Galatians 2:20). The life we now live in the body, we live not according to the without-God impulses and drives to which it has been habituated, but rather in learning to trust the Father like Jesus trusted the Father for everything he needed. We live in a kingdom of love and generosity, not of selfishness or greed. We live in the same trust in God that guided and moved Jesus. These are the impulses to which we give attention and respond. This is a way to recognize and lean into unholy resistance.

Another helpful concept to remember is that our life in Christ does not begin with initiating and doing good things. "I would like to learn just one thing from you: Did you receive the Spirit by the works of the law, or by believing what you heard? Are you so foolish? After beginning by means of the Spirit, are you now trying to finish by means of the flesh?" (Galatians 3:2-3). We do not generate life but express life in the good that we do. Life is a gift, not a paycheck. What is begun by God through the Spirit can only be continued in God through the Spirit. And it is the desires inspired by the Spirit within us that will move us in this direction. This helps us put the resistance that arises from our flesh in perspective. It is always moving us away from our goal of wholeness.

Further along in Galatians, Paul writes, "My dear children, for whom I am again in the pains of childbirth until Christ is formed in you" (Galatians 4:19). This language about a mother giving birth to a child resonates when we think about our own transformation and that of others we care about: we want Christ to be more fully formed in us. Resistance would hinder us from realizing this holy goal. Our lives become de-formed by letting the world around us squeeze us into its shape. They also become de-formed by our resistance to the good into which we are invited.

Instead of being trapped in a state of resistance, remember this: "You, my brothers and sisters, were called to be free. But do not use your freedom to indulge the flesh; rather, serve one an-other humbly in love" (Galatians 5:13). The freedom with which we have been made free in relationship with God through Christ (such good news!) is lost if we spend it under the management of our without-God resistances and impulses. If we let resistance make our decisions for us, we will not find ourselves growing in freedom. Resistance traps me. I find myself less free, even en-slaved to a phantom me. But freedom lived in love under the Spirit's guidance and empowerment grows and flourishes.

How does this work? Instead of listening to and following our own resistance, we can remember this counsel: "Walk by the Spirit, and you will not gratify the desires of the flesh. For the flesh desires what is contrary to the Spirit, and the Spirit what is contrary to the flesh. They are in conflict with each other, so that you are not to do whatever you want. But if you are led by the Spirit, you are not under the law" (Galatians 5:16-18).

What the resistance embedded in my old self seeks and what the Spirit seeks are in conflict. The scriptural language is "the flesh resists the Spirit." We can't live by the impulses of the flesh and be in step with the Spirit any more than we can turn both left and right at an intersection. The resistance that rises in me is not seeking to move me in the direction of God's good for me. This is why we learn to notice resisting impulses, and then lean into them in keeping with what the Spirit invites us into.

> If we let resistance make our decisions for us, we will not find ourselves growing in freedom.

What shape does my own resistance take in me? We can recognize some of its bad fruit in this list: "The acts of the flesh are obvious: sexual immorality, impurity and debauchery; idolatry and witchcraft; hatred, discord, jealousy, fits of rage, selfish ambition, dissensions, factions and envy; drunkenness, orgies, and the like. I warn you, as I did before, that those who live like this will not inherit the kingdom of God" (Galatians 5:19-21).

If we let the impulses and inclinations of our human resistance to good guide our lives and make our decisions for us, we end up with a lot of unhelpful, unhealthy, and unholy realities in our behavior, relationships, and outcomes. When followed, these make us less and less at home in the kingdom of

God. Resistance doesn't want to be at home there. If what we want is to enter into the kingdom of God, both now and into our future forever, we don't want to follow the voice of inward resistance. That does not lead to a path of life. This is why we take resistance seriously.

People in this world who aren't interested in the life of God think that they've found life when they live for human pleasure, human power, human purposes, and human priorities *alone*. "This is the life," they say. But the trajectory of this path is never in the direction of sustainability or lasting vitality or growing joy or deep peace and meaning. These are only found in communion with God. And human resistance, by definition, is not at home in the presence of God.

When, however, we learn to press through resistance and follow Spirit-inspired desire, we find a beautiful, welcome sort of fruitfulness: "But the fruit of the Spirit is love, joy, peace, forbearance, kindness, goodness, faithfulness, gentleness and self-control. Against such things there is no law" (Galatians 5:22-23). A life lived in communion with God by following the desires of the Spirit leads to a quality of life very much at home in the kingdom of God. Living by the Spirit—in communion with God rather than in resistance to God—allows us to experience the reality of the kingdom here and now. This isn't just a "heaven when you die" reality, but a trajectory of living reality now. It is a path on which we make progress in life-giving, joyful ways of well-being, well-living, and well-serving.

So when it comes to acting in regard to the resistance that rises up within us, these words help: "Those who belong to Christ Jesus have crucified the flesh with its passions and desires. Since we live by the Spirit, let us keep in step with the Spirit. Let us not become conceited, provoking and envying each other" (Galatians 5:24-26).

What do we do with the resistance that arises within us in the form of passions, desires, inclinations, and disinclinations? We let all of that die on the cross with Christ. We let it die so that, by the Spirit, we might truly live—risen, like Christ. Our problem arises when we imagine our resistance as the most alive thing about us, when the opposite is actually true. Walking with the Spirit leads us on a journey in which we can be guided and empowered by the life of God. It can be a pathway of transformation more and more into the image of God we see in Jesus.

So how does overcoming resistance work in community? "Brothers and sisters, if someone is caught in a sin, you who live by the Spirit should restore that person gently. But watch yourselves, or you also may be tempted. Carry each other's burdens, and in this way you will fulfill the law of Christ" (Galatians 6:1-2). In context, this is a statement about how those who are walking in the Spirit and bearing the fruit of God's kingdom should respond to someone who is caught up in a life dominated by their own resistance to God. These friends are caught. They are trapped. They are slaves. They are *not* free. If we are trying to live in resistance to our own resistance, we will want to help others enter into the same freedom. We never hold another in contempt, because we are just as susceptible to our own resistance as another. Rather, we live with love toward others just as Christ came to live in love among us.

It helps to remember the reality of following our own resistances: "Do not be deceived: God cannot be mocked. A man reaps what he sows. Whoever sows to please their flesh, from the flesh will reap destruction; whoever sows to please the Spirit, from the Spirit will reap eternal life. Let us not become weary in doing good, for at the proper time we will reap a harvest if we do not give up" (Galatians 6:7-9).

We are sometimes deceived about the nature of reality. If we allow our resistance to become our primary reality, we find we're fooling ourselves and failing to live in divine reality. If we keep letting resistance that arises from within us make our decisions and guide our steps, it is no surprise where we end up. We enjoy real life less and less. Our decisions and our actions are growing something unhelpful (at best). Instead, we would rather have an abundant harvest of the good life. So, we keep learning how to plant attentiveness and responsiveness to what the Spirit wants in us and for us.

OPPORTUNITY FOR GROWTH

Abbot David Geraets was the founder of a School for Spiritual Directors and the Abbot of the Monastery of the Risen Christ, a charismatic Catholic community. When I (Gem) was in the process of being trained as a spiritual director, I had the treat of meeting with Abbot David as my spiritual director. This was a far cry from the Protestant, non-denominational church experience I had enjoyed for most of my life. My time with that community enriched and enlivened my life with God in ways I never knew possible. Abbot David (along with the rest of the community) opened my eyes to so many of the inner dynamics of my soul. I came upon them at just the right time in my transformational process. I was squarely in mid-life, and I was ready to fully engage in that excruciating season of being completely undone. I say that so blithely right now because, truthfully, I had no idea what I was in for at that time.

One idea that Abbot David uttered repeatedly gave me a new vision for transformation: "Any place of resistance in your life is your next opportunity for growth." I didn't know it then, but from that point forward, for quite a few years, I would engage many points of resistance and, yes, I would grow, painfully and steadily so. How do you continue to cooperate with your transformational process when resistance, by definition, keeps you from moving forward?

I grew up on six acres in a small town in Washington. My dad worked a full-time job in town and also single handedly took care of all six acres. He mowed the pastures by hand using a device that had two rows of interlocking scissor-like teeth (no riding mower for him). He also tended three gardens on the main section of our property surrounding our home. We had a flower garden with all of my mom's favorite flowers, including iris, daffodils, and gladiolas. Our second garden contained vegetables like carrots, corn, and green beans. The third garden was spread with low-lying vine produce such as squash, pumpkin, and watermelon, and was lined with the most fragrant lilac bushes. Our yard was a cornucopia of produce and beauty.

My dad planned, roto-tilled, fertilized, planted, watered, and cared for all of the gardens. I could say I helped with the gardening, but only like a six-year-old "helps" you carry your luggage through an airport. My part was small but fun. He would give me a handful of seeds and say, "Okay, now, use your finger to make a hole, drop two to three seeds in it, cover it gently, and repeat." I would get on my hands and knees in that rich, dark soil and make little girl finger-sized holes. I was careful to put just the right amount of seeds into the holes before I moved on. It was wonderful time spent with my dad.

My little process of planting seeds helped us along toward building a garden. And even though my dad bought the seeds, prepared the soil, planted, and watered, neither I nor my dad actually grew the plants. Nature, as intended by God, did its work. Seeds opened and sent down little roots, plants grew, vegetables developed, and then we ate the fruit of our labor. In the same way, God is the one who grows and transforms us. All of the spiritual practices we participate in are merely the planting of the seeds, the tilling of the soil, the watering of the plants. God is the one who grows the fruit of the Spirit in our lives. In overcoming resistance, our job is to get ourselves into God's presence so that he may do his good work in us and then through us. It is him that we seek.

If you want to be the kind of person who cooperates and allows the real adventures of life to do their work in you, what could you do? Begin by noticing and cooperating with what God is allowing in your life to shape and form you. Continue to let go of the false self and embrace your true self. The answer lies more in *cooperation* than in direct action. Gerald May, in his book *Simply Sane*, notes:

> True growth is a process one allows to happen rather than causes to happen. A seed grows into a plant because it is its nature to do so, not because you or I cause it to grow. If a seed finds itself in rich earth, with reasonable quantities of water and sunlight, growth will happen. If we sprinkle the ground with fertilizer, water it regularly and keep pests away, we become involved in the growth process, and growth may be stronger and richer. We are participating in the growth, but we are still not causing it.[2]

In other words, we do not actually grow plants. We till the ground, fertilize the soil, plant the seeds, and water the garden. But we are unable to grow a plant. We make the environment conducive to growth. That is what the spiritual practices and our own inner work are for. That is what a life of process is about.

A POSTURE FOR TRANSFORMATION

I've long been intrigued by process, and, paired with my natural bent toward curiosity, I paused once to ask God how my life's journey had brought me to that current point. Of course, I could look back and see how I had imperfectly and messily traversed all of the circumstances in my life—the highs, the lows, and the in-betweens. But what propelled me forward before, during, and after each season, keeping in mind the dynamics of a life of transformation? How did I make my way through resistance?

As I pondered my journey, the first three dynamics that arose from within were the words *open, aware,* and *willing.*[3]

Open: Do you want it? Openness implies receptivity, the opposite of being closed up, small, narrow, and the attitude "I don't need that." We don't have to be perfectly open. God welcomes us at our current state of readiness. However, at any point, we can decide to become even just a bit more open so that we can welcome whatever is next. Throughout every season of our lives, it is possible to be open and listen to God's voice and follow his promptings.

This means having the courage to stretch beyond what feels safe. Any real change requires leaving the safety of where we are to venture into new territory. How much do you want transformation that leads to greater freedom? Engaging with an open heart and mind can keep the pathway clear.

Aware: Are you noticing? After identifying a sense of being open, the next dynamic to emerge is awareness. This begs the question of having access to a higher consciousness. We can call this part of ourselves the "inner observer." The inner observer allows us to stand back a bit and get a more objective look at what is going on. When we don't engage the inner observer, we can get stuck in reactive mode.

With our inner observer engaged we can notice more often what is going on inside of us which, in turn, can lead to insights that lead to healing. Awareness takes as much courage as openness because we are saying that we are not afraid to dig deeper into our inner world. We are not afraid to tackle our weaknesses and issues. We are not afraid to notice what is occurring in our relationships and take appropriate action for change.

Willing: Are you willing to take action? Right on the heels of being open and aware, we find willingness. Are we willing to do something about what we have been open to and the inner dynamics we found as we became more aware? This is an important moment. If we are not willing to take action, then, by definition, we will remain behind the wall of resistance.

Being open, aware, and willing is the place to begin if we find ourselves stuck in resistance. Each word is invitational and implies gracious presence with ourselves and others.

We may be tempted to weariness when it comes to being attentive and responsive to God in the face of resistance. But when we choose to lean in despite the tiredness, it always leads to an abundant harvest of life. Resistance is, in part, the temptation to give in to our "I don't feel like it" urges when we don't see the good fruit of our Spirit-inspired steps borne immediately.

Perhaps the most simple and clear statement about resistance comes in these words: "May I never boast except in the cross of our Lord Jesus Christ, through which the world has been crucified to me, and I to the world" (Galatians 6:14). There is a powerful dynamic in the cross of Christ that enables us to live free of every resistant impulse within us that would lead us along a path of deformation rather than under the guidance of God's Spirit that leads to transformation.

Noticing and paying attention to the resistances that arise within us is good spiritual work. Continue to ask yourself, "Where am I saying, 'No, thanks' to God? Where does resistance rise up in me?"

A key to working with our resistance is the word *through*. We have to work *through* the resistance once we notice it. Denial or covering it up keeps us stuck and won't work long term. We have found sometimes we were not willing to move beyond certain resistance points until the pain of *not* moving through them became greater than the pain of leaning in to them. For self-protection, we tend to stay with familiar pain to avoid unfamiliar pain. Yet we can find the courage to acknowledge our resistance points and do our best to graciously move through them.

> Continue to ask yourself, "Where am I saying, 'No, thanks' to God? Where does resistance rise up in me?"

BE TRANSFORMED

1. In what area of your life do you sense the most resistance?

2. Describe what it feels like and how you desire to move forward.

3. What does it look like these days as you plan, roto-till, fertilize, plant, water, and care for the garden of your soul?

4. Where do you find yourself in the process of being *open, aware, and willing*?

5. What might it take to grow or move along in this process?

4

VULNERABILITY

WHERE ARE YOU HIDING?

Grace—*Grace is abundantly given by God, yet sometimes we have a hard time receiving this grace. We also have a hard time giving ourselves grace. Most people we talk with have a very hard time with this. Learn to be especially gracious in your self-talk. And, as often as possible, speak grace to others. Our culture can be rather harsh at times, and we all need grace. As we receive grace from God, we take it in for ourselves and then we can more easily grant grace to others.*

WE WEREN'T A CHURCH-GOING FAMILY when I (Alan) was growing up, but for some season I attended Sunday school at a local church that I now recognize as being on the fundamentalist end of the spectrum. What I remember is that they caused me to be afraid of God. They managed to turn Psalm 139 into bad news. You know that wonderful verse that says, "Where can

I go from your Spirit? Where can I flee from your presence?" It's very comforting in context. This church had a different way of interpreting that line: "No matter where you run, God will always find you!"

I was terrified. I remember deciding in my child-like mind that there was a particular hydrangea bush in my backyard next to a fence that was somehow the one place where I could safely hide from God. I'm not sure why I thought this particular variety of bush would promise to be some sort of divine kryptonite, but I couldn't live with the idea of that kind of God finding me no matter where I went.

This established a habit of hiding that, even after I came to trust the true God revealed in Jesus Christ, continued to be a place of struggle. For different reasons, many of us have developed a habit of hiding. It's a very human condition.

> Many of us have developed a habit of hiding.

I've avoided vulnerability and put up walls of self-protection when I feared that, instead of a Protector and a good heavenly Father, God was a dangerous presence. The problem is that the walls I put up to protect me became a barrier to the kind of transformation that I truly and deeply desire. It helped to learn that I am safe in the presence of God. I don't need my self-made protections.

Many of us struggle with being vulnerable. We live in a world that exploits vulnerability. But in the presence of God, we need not put up protective barriers. We can open ourselves to God fully. Whatever is in our hearts and minds is perfectly safe to raise in the light of God's loving presence. Whatever is broken can be restored in the light. Whatever is soiled can be cleansed in the light. Whatever is bent can be made straight in the light.

This is how we can come to understand walking in the light. It is not a Pharisee-like "always looking good" dynamic. It is an honest, open way of living our lives, shortcomings and all, in the presence of God.

AN UNEXPECTED DOORWAY

No one was more surprised than me (Gem) to learn that our dog, Lex, would be the doorway to a new level of vulnerability. Our youngest son had been begging for a dog for many years. And I kept thinking, and may have said aloud, "Why in the world would I want a dog in my life? We have three sons. Isn't that enough activity and mess?" I saw a dog as a perpetual toddler that would only make more work for me.

But when our youngest was ten years old, and after practicing with two hamsters and a chameleon, I was finally ready to say yes to a dog. Our two younger sons and I were the first to visit the local shelter to rescue the perfect pet for our family. We entered a large, covered, open-ended building full of various breeds. The barking noises were deafening as we were beckoned to each cage. On our left was a tiny, wide-eyed Chihuahua named Connor who shivered at the sight of us. Too tiny. Up ahead was a beautiful cocker spaniel named Belle and a husky-dalmation mix named Sneaker. Too large. But one dog caught our attention in his own unique way. We looked down on our right to see a small, tan Greyhuahua named Lex. Lex didn't utter a sound. He merely stood with his paws on the lowest rail of his enclosure and looked up at us longingly with his deep, dark brown eyes. That was it. All three of us were goners. We planned for Alan and our older son to visit and to make our final decision. Afterward, we all agreed: Lex was our dog.

We took Lex home and were acclimating him to our environment. After seeing how happy our new pet clearly made all of us, our youngest exclaimed, "I told you! We could have been feeling this way for years!" We laughed with him in his exuberance.

Even though Lex was supposed to be our son's dog, he quickly decided that I was his person. This was solidified when, just two months after we rescued him from the shelter, I entered into my "summer of pain." The entire time I was convalescing from severe nerve pain, Lex stayed right by my side. He was a sweet presence in the midst of traumatic physical suffering and, from that time on, we were bonded.

Lex shined a light on a level of feeling that I had apparently lost connection with long ago. I came to recognize this as an invitation to another level of vulnerability. At the time, I thought I was open. Socially I am relatively caring and hospitable. Among my friends I am known as guileless and friendly, but over time I began to see that deep inside, I had erected a wall to keep myself safe. It was so carefully placed that even I didn't know it was there.

It was odd to acknowledge this as I considered myself a person who easily talked about my life and heart issues. But this new sense of tenderness I had for Lex showed me that, at some point, I had closed deeper levels of myself off and created a kind of barrier around my heart. When I saw how deeply I could feel connected to another "being" it scared me. It seemed to me to be an open door to being more deeply hurt.

The barrier, I discovered, was a kind of protection that kept me safe from people's expectations. After spending the next few years (after adopting Lex) doing the hard work in counseling of finding my voice and learning healthy boundaries, I knew that I was not responsible for others. I didn't have to be afraid of what they would "take" from me. Being vulnerable does not make me a victim. I give what I want and I say no if I need to (inwardly and outwardly). But with voice and boundaries intact, I was still left with the old pattern of inwardly protecting.

I am a bit embarrassed to say that a dog made me aware of some of my vulnerability issues. Wouldn't it be more romantic if I said that directly upon meeting Alan, he broke down all of my walls and barriers in one fell swoop and I was forever open and healed? But it didn't work that way. I had learned to erect walls of protection over the course of my growing-up years through family experiences as well as unhelpful interactions in school that most of us are familiar with. My connection to Lex was a gift from God, who showed me over time that I still had some walls up.

NOTICING THE SELF-PROTECTIVE STANCE

I've become aware, again, of this erected wall, protecting me from vulnerability. But, by God's grace, he is still leading me toward greater health and wholeness, which I whole-heartedly welcome. So, if I'm going to tackle another layer in this regard, God has my full attention. As I've become aware of this place of protection, I've been practicing *noticing it* and *keeping it soft*. Let me explain.

EXERCISE

When I see myself going into a self-protective stance (which undermines my vulnerability), I take a moment to notice any negative self-talk about myself, another person, or the situation. Then I make the decision to quell that negative voice. I tend toward mind reading, presuming, and assuming, so learning to let go of others and their thoughts and responses has been quite freeing.

Once I've noticed my self-protection and spoken to it, I then notice where I am feeling the tension in my body. I picture invulnerability as being a hard surface, like a plexiglass wall. When it comes to vulnerability, I usually feel that tension in the space between my heart and my belly. So I pause, physically relax my belly, and breathe into it. This is what I mean by "keeping it soft." I've learned that my tension is tied to the energy it takes to keep that wall up, to deflect and protect.

In *Surrender to Love*, David Benner states, "Daring to accept myself and receive love for who I am in my nakedness and vulnerability is the indispensable precondition for genuine transformation."[1] As I continue to learn that I am perfectly safe in the kingdom of God, I realize that I don't need to protect myself nearly as often as I've thought. Vulnerability keeps me on the way of transformation.

DISCOVERING LOVE AND EMPATHY

Once I had access to that soft place within myself, in its unprotected state, I realized that others may still be trapped behind the walls they had erected in self-protection. I felt compassion for them. Empathy was one of the first emotions to rise up once I was more in touch with my vulnerable self. Brené Brown, in her book *Daring Greatly*, says, "Vulnerability is the birthplace of love, belonging, joy, courage, empathy, and creativity. It is the source of hope, empathy, accountability, and authenticity. If we want greater clarity in our purpose or deeper and more meaningful spiritual lives, vulnerability is the path."[2]

I also found that I was open to more love. I could receive people as they are and with the love and relationship they were offering.

The wall of invulnerability not only keeps me hidden, but it keeps the fullness of experienced love out. The joy is to let love be what it is. To not put parameters on another person's ability to love me. This has helped tremendously in my marriage and friendships.

In *No Man Is an Island*, Thomas Merton penetrates our hearts with his pointed prose: "The beginning of love is the will to let those we love be perfectly themselves, the resolution not to twist them to fit our own image. If in loving them we do not love what they are, but only their potential likeness to ourselves, then we do not love them: we only love the reflection of ourselves we find in them."[3] The risk of becoming vulnerable opened to me the path described by Merton. As I stand firmly in the love of God, without fear and hiding, I am more able to let others be who they are. I don't need to see myself in them; I can let them be them. And I get to be me. And we get to love each other in that beautiful space.

RAW IS BETTER

When you have a DSLR (digital single-lens reflex) camera you can choose to shoot your images in either RAW or JPG mode. All images are made up of pixels. Pixels are like tiny dots all scrunched together to make the image that you see when you look at a photo. If you were to magnify down into an image you would see something like figure 1.

A JPG image compresses some of the pixels together when you take the picture. It might take all of the whites in one section of the image and combine them together, and it

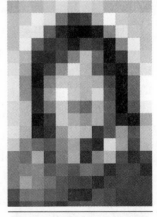

Figure 1. Close-up view of pixels

might combine all of the red pixels from another section. This means you do not have access to all of the pixels when you edit the photo, which means there is less ability to fix a mistake or enhance an image.

A RAW image is taken in such a way that every single pixel in an image retains the ability to be manipulated or enhanced when you edit the photo. Each pixel remains independent of the others. Having used RAW mode, you could correct mistakes you made when you snapped the image. You have access to every single pixel. This is great news if you take an underexposed photo and need to brighten it. With the touch of a slider, you can bring a dark photo into the light.

It may feel horrible, but being raw in your own life of transformation can be similarly good. You have access to everything you need to become everything you could be. Being raw looks like being vulnerable or acknowledging that sometimes you don't have the answers. It can mean being honest about what is actually happening rather than sliding into denial. Being raw can also mean not rationalizing or making something pretty that isn't pretty.

I won't lie, remaining raw takes courage. Courage because the process for true healing usually takes time, and sustained courage during that process can be very difficult. But remember, RAW mode leaves the image (and you) open to the most enhancing. And if you want God to continue his work of transformation, then keeping yourself open is totally worth it.

On the flip side, leaving yourself closed, going into denial, and rationalizing can all keep you in JPG mode. You might be moving along, but the deepest work isn't being accessed because your openness level is compressed or shallow. In an online article, Richard Rohr shares,

Did you ever imagine that what we call "vulnerability" might just be the key to ongoing growth? In my experience, healthily vulnerable people use every occasion to expand, change, and grow. Yet it is a risky position to live undefended, in a kind of constant openness to the other—because it means others could sometimes actually wound us. Indeed, *vulnera* comes from the Latin for "to wound." But only if we take this risk do we also allow the opposite possibility: the other might also gift us, free us, and even love us.[4]

Are you experiencing a RAW place right now? Even though it hurts and you just want it to be over, try taking a moment to see the beauty of having full access to the change that needs to occur. Like an image in the hand of a skilled photographer, you have access to every single inner pixel. You are open. Being raw and vulnerable allows for that. Once you have decided to take some steps in becoming more vulnerable, there are three relationships in which you can begin to practice the enhancing.

Counseling. Counseling is a wonderful place to begin the process of vulnerability. We both feel fortunate to have been in the hands of a gifted and experienced counselor. The nuances of vulnerability we are able to work on now are only possible because we took the time to share every nook and cranny of our lives that needed healing. Both transgressions and wounds have been laid out and examined one by one. Healing comes at the end of each situation because of the process as a whole.

If you haven't yet stepped into counseling for various reasons, one being fear, let us encourage you—it is worth it. No matter your age or stage, now is the time. If you work the process all the way through, you will see the fruit of your labor. The freedom that is possible may be unimaginable, but it is real. Your

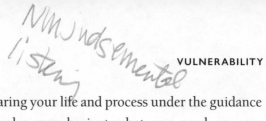

vulnerability in sharing your life and process under the guidance of a skilled counselor may be just what you need on your journey of transformation.

Spiritual direction. Our spiritual directors have been wonderful listeners and have taught us many things over the years. We are thankful for the gift of these people in our lives. In the trustworthy presence of a spiritual director you can practice being vulnerable and sharing your life, your soul. Here are three ways a spiritual director can help you share openly.

First, one of the hallmarks of good spiritual directors is their ability to listen well. This involves not merely listening but being present while listening. In this way, a spiritual director becomes a kind of holy container for your thoughts, ideas, yearnings, and stories. You get to hear your own voice in a nonjudgmental atmosphere. The spiritual director may bring some insight, but the act of you bringing your soul out into the light in vulnerability gets you halfway there (or more).

Second, a spiritual director helps us to hold the big picture of our personal story. It is surprising each time a spiritual director reminds us of something we said months or years ago. They can connect the dots by showing you how what you are saying now connects to a part of your story from the past. Sometimes we are too close to the situation to see the big picture. The spiritual director helps you get up into the helicopter and see the full view, which can remind you of your growth over time or bring to life a long-held desire. A trustworthy person who keeps the long view of your life in focus is a great gift.

Finally, a director is a person who does not judge. They may ask, "Why are you judging that?" This comes up when we are making statements about ourselves that are less than encouraging.

The question can pop you back to reality and usually leaves us wordless. You can pause and ask yourself again, "Why *am* I judging that?" Judgment is a surefire way to stop growth in its tracks. You cannot flourish under the weight of judgment. Discernment is one thing, judgment is another. What a gift it has been to learn, over time, to stop judging ourselves (and others) so that we can make our way to more vulnerability and more freedom.

> Judgment is a surefire way to stop growth in its tracks. You cannot flourish under the weight of judgment.

Spiritual friendship. Spiritual friends are those with whom we have an intimate relationship, sharing our highs, our lows, our fears, our dreams, our wrestling places. We do not judge each other. We listen. We talk. We encourage. We add insight if it strikes. We ask questions. The basic details of *what* and *who* certainly enter the conversation, but we share beneath the surface of all of that. We engage our souls.

We all need places to throw out our doubts and fears and have someone look at them in a caring, loving manner. There may be a place in my life where the light isn't shining bright enough. The situation is not in focus and I am in the dark on how to proceed. I can't seem to get a clear view on things. Being vulnerable, talking it out, and having someone listen can usually bring its own clarity. Light emerges, my surroundings come into focus, and I can see things more as they really are. My situations are not fully solved, but I walk away a little more focused and with more discernment than when I began.

Do yourself a favor. Call a friend, get a date on the calendar, and then listen to each other. Be as vulnerable as you can and give each other the gift of listening without judging or solving. Dig beneath the surface and build each other up.

THE HABIT OF HIDING

We often work with Christian leaders in many different organizational environments. Unfortunately, doing what we do, we've seen a lot of leaders fall. In nearly every case, these leaders had developed a strong habit of hiding. They grew to pretend more and more in the presence of even those closest to them. They were afraid to be vulnerable, even though this would have been the very doorway to freedom and transformation. They settled for looking transformed rather than being transformed.

> We have a hard time coupling vulnerability and authority, but kingdom authority is good friends with vulnerability.

We have a hard time coupling vulnerability and authority, but kingdom authority is good friends with vulnerability. It is in the kingdoms of this world that the two seem like oil and water. David Bosch, South African missiologist and theologian, in talking about the authority of Paul the apostle, writes:

> Being unknown, dying, disciplined, in sorrow and poverty are the true marks of an apostle. Weakness is an authentic characteristic of the apostolic ministry. Without the weakness which [Paul's] opponents deride, there can be no real apostolic ministry and no true proclamation of Christ. The church is not made up of spiritual giants; only broken [people] can lead others to the cross. It is on [people] like Peter that Jesus builds His church. The possibility of change and conversion is based on humans being vulnerable; it does not, however, involve the vulnerability only of the one whom we would like to convert but also our own vulnerability as missionaries. Jesus revealed what sin is only because He Himself had been vulnerable; had

He opted for invulnerability the true nature of sin would have remained hidden.[5]

Vulnerability is needed not only on the part of the one who would receive the gospel but also on the part of the one who would proclaim it. Only the broken can lead others to the cross. Without brokenness, how can we understand grace? And how can kingdom influence happen apart from divine grace?

In his book *Strong and Weak*, author Andy Crouch helps us understand that human flourishing happens when both authority and vulnerability are strong and present. He exposes our tendency to assume that these are in an either-or relationship to one another. Vulnerability is not weakness. And authority is not merely about human strength.[6]

We find great hope as we interact with young and emerging leaders about these things. We find a much greater readiness to live in the fruitful intersection of vulnerability and authority. In recent years, we have enjoyed spending time with a group of young influencers. We often share honestly about the bumps and detours we've taken along the way in our own lives and work. We find an easy honesty coming back to us in response. Again, vulnerability can be scary, but it is a place of substantial kingdom transformation.

Recently, we were taking a walk and a metaphor arose for how hiding feels and how vulnerability helps. I (Alan) find that when I default to familiar hiding, my mind and heart are like a closed-up, dark shack with all the windows shut and shuttered. The air grows stale. Unwelcome things grow in the dark. I find myself embarrassed, even ashamed, of this dark, dingy space, and so I'm tempted to leave the doors and windows shut.

But whenever I open the door, even a crack, and open the shutters to let in a little light and air, it always helps. I talk with a good friend about the stale thoughts that have been crowding my heart and mind. I acknowledge places of unresisted temptation and subsequent guilt and shame. This can also happen in a place of honest, vulnerable prayer. I let the light of kingdom reality pour into my dark heart and mind. I let the breeze of God's presence blow through and displace the dank air that had been filling it. The challenge is to leave the doors and windows open. I still have a habit of hiding. I still resist vulnerability. But vulnerability is the way to fresh air and a lighter heart.

When I rise in the morning in a dark mood, it's as though the doors and windows have shut overnight. At that point I can autopilot my way through the day, stuck again in this dark and dank space. Or I can open my heart and my mind before the Father of light. I can welcome the truth and reality of who God is and how I am welcome in his presence. I can bring my anxiety into the presence of the Prince of Peace. I can bring my fears to the One who is a safe refuge. I can bring my doubting into the presence of the One who treated Thomas's doubts so gently. I can let the psalm writers guide me with their wise and vulnerable prayers.

Sometimes, opening the doors and windows of my soul looks like confession. I've done or said what I wish I hadn't. I didn't do or say what I wish I had. Confession is telling it like it actually is and how God already sees it. It's agreeing with God rather than pretending or putting on a mask.

Think of the confession psalms of David. We're grateful for the first few lines of Psalm 51, for example:

Have mercy on me, O God,
    according to your unfailing love;
according to your great compassion
    blot out my transgressions.
Wash away all my iniquity
    and cleanse me from my sin.
For I know my transgressions,
    and my sin is always before me.
Against you, you only, have I sinned
    and done what is evil in your sight;
so you are right in your verdict
    and justified when you judge. (Psalm 51:1-4)

Like David, we are well aware of the lines we've crossed. Our shortcomings are real. David's words express what is in our hearts as well. But God doesn't want to hold our shortcomings or our line crossings against us. God would much rather blot these things out, wash them away, and breathe fresh wind into our thoughts and intentions.

Confession isn't about lingering in the place of guilt and shame in the presence of an offended God. It is acknowledging the real causes of guilt in the presence of a God whose bias is toward mercy and grace. We have a loving and compassionate God. That's where David begins. That's where confession happens. And confession frees us to continue our transforming journey.

Too often, we may be tempted to assume that God is as critical of us as we tend to be of ourselves. But does God take delight in judgment or in mercy (Micah 7:18)? Does God let anger drive him to reject us, or does he actually long to be gracious to us (Isaiah 30:18)? The good news is that God sent his Son into the world to save it and not to condemn it (John 3:17). Each of us is a part of that world God loves. It is good to be honest in the presence of such a God.

In another of David's psalms of confession, he proclaims the good news of God's forgiving ways. Confession is vulnerable honesty about what we've not done well and what we've left undone.

> Blessed is the one
>> whose transgressions are forgiven,
>> whose sins are covered.
> Blessed is the one
>> whose sin the LORD does not count against them
>> and in whose spirit is no deceit. (Psalm 32:1-2)

Those who are forgiven know they are blessed. Confessional vulnerability is a path to living in such a place of blessing. The last thing God wants is to be separate from us. God has done all he can to bring us close. The Lord does not desire or intend to hold our sins against us. He asks only that we be honest about the reality of our shortcomings. Such honesty is a way of walking in the light of his presence. What he can't forgive is our pretending, because the pretender doesn't seek forgiveness. The pretender keeps silent and remains invulnerable.

> When I kept silent,
>> my bones wasted away
>> through my groaning all day long.
> For day and night
>> your hand was heavy on me;
> my strength was sapped
>> as in the heat of summer. (Psalm 32:3-4)

When we keep silent, our security, confidence, and courage wane. Instead of blessing comes groaning morning, noon, and night. We feel God's presence as heaviness because we don't want him to look into what we're hiding (as though he could not see what we hide; what we think of as hiding is self-deception). When we keep silent, our strength and energy are sapped as on a hot afternoon. Pretending nothing's wrong only gives what's wrong more power. What is unholy only grows in the dark.

> Then I acknowledged my sin to you
>   and did not cover up my iniquity.
> I said, "I will confess
>   my transgressions to the LORD."
> And you forgave
>   the guilt of my sin. (Psalm 32:5)

When we become vulnerable in the merciful light of God's loving presence, when we acknowledge the reality of what we've done and not done, said and not said, then we will experience the light and freshness of forgiveness. Then, kingdom confidence, security, strength, energy, and joy begin to return to us.

> Therefore let all the faithful pray to you
>   while you may be found;
> surely the rising of the mighty waters
>   will not reach them.
> You are my hiding place;
>   you will protect me from trouble
>   and surround me with songs of deliverance.
> I will instruct you and teach you in the way you should go;
>   I will counsel you with my loving eye on you.
>   (Psalm 32:6-8)

Being honest and open in the presence of God allows us to live in the light of God's good, beautiful, and true kingdom. We find a high place above the rising mighty waters. We find a hiding place in the place of trouble. We feel songs of deliverance surrounding us. We experience God as our loving guide, teacher, and counselor. God cannot guide us, teach us, or counsel us if we are hiding, not because he is unable, but because we are unavailable.

In the place of soul honesty in the Presence, we experience God's "I will." We sense God's being for us—seeking and working for our good. When we are closed up with our guilt and shame, we presume God to be all about those things as well. We miss the gentle, quiet reality of God's determined care for each of us.

The invitation is to be one of the faithful ones who pray to God in every moment in which we find ourselves awake to God with us. When mighty waters of fear, anxiety, insecurity, or doubt rise to threaten us, they will not overwhelm us (even reach us) because we will have found a safe and protected place in God.

So, vulnerability is opening up our lives and bringing them into the light. But we only open up when we feel safe. We can open up in the presence of God because God is safe. In *The Lion, the Witch and the Wardrobe* by C. S. Lewis, Mr. Beaver tells Susan that Aslan isn't safe. He's good, but not safe. Perhaps he's saying that Aslan isn't tame, or even predictable—but he is good. We can be vulnerable in the presence of God because God is good. He may not be predictable. He may do things that surprise or even startle us, but he is always working for what is truly good in our lives.

BE TRANSFORMED

1. What are some ways in which you have been afraid to be vulnerable before God? With yourself? With others?

2. Describe how you have made your way to vulnerability in the past. How might those ways help you become more vulnerable now? How does the idea of staying raw help?

3. Notice an area of your life that feels like a dark shack. What would it look like for you to open a window or two or even the door? What freedoms might occur if you shared this space with a trusted friend?

4. How has God become your hiding place?

5

TRUTH

WHAT IS MOST REAL TO YOU?

Notice—*This is such a gentle word and one of my favorites. It's quiet and graceful. Whatever the issue, simply see it. Don't judge it. The word notice is especially helpful when working with desires or weaknesses. Gentle seeing leads to discernment and then more hopeful change.*

Discern—*Discerning involves not only the mind but also the heart. You can rely on past experiences and wise counsel. Discerning makes space for thoughtful reflection and not just knee-jerk reactions or simply a list of pros and cons. It's about responding rather than reacting. When the moment for a decision comes, discernment keeps the relationality of that decision intact.*

WHEN I (GEM) WAS ABOUT FIVE YEARS OLD, my mom and I enjoyed a road trip from Washington to California to visit my grandparents. At one point during the long drive, I decided to take a nap. I had eaten my lunch, except for a few potato chips in a little yellow bag. I put them up on the dashboard and went to sleep.

When I woke up, I checked my chip bag for a snack, and all of the chips were gone. I asked my mom where my chips were. She told me that sometimes when you leave potato chips out in the sun, they disintegrate and disappear. I questioned her, but she insisted, so I believed her.

Many years later, newly married and in my twenties, I was on a road trip with Alan. I was staring out the front window and my eyes drifted down to the dashboard. I recalled that road trip with my mom and how the potato chips disappeared. It was then that I realized, wait a minute! Chips can't disappear! My mom *ate* those chips! At this point, of course, I was laughing out loud, yelling, "The sun doesn't make chips disintegrate!" I then had the chance to tell Alan the story and we laughed together.

So, now that you know that I am one of the most gullible people on the planet, a few questions bubble up to the surface: What other beliefs have I picked up over the course of my life are not true, even though I still act like they are? Am I willing to go on a search for the actual truth? Am I willing to dig down inside myself to find deeper truths than I currently know exist? This willingness to search for truth is another path to transformation.

God is absolutely trustworthy. He does not lie, trick, or tease. When God says, "I love you," I can simply take that at face value and let that be my reality. I can sink into his love and then move out into my life from that home base. When God says,

"Do not be afraid," I can rest in his words. I can trust that he actually does know what is best for me right now, even though I can't see it.

IT'S ABOUT THE TRUTH

"How did that happen?" I asked my counselor in one of my final appointments. I had fully participated in my own healing process under the guidance of this skilled and gifted counselor. At the same time, I was amazed, as I not only experienced but also watched myself become free in ways I had never imagined. So I was looking for a key, a secret or some magical explanation. My counselor simply said, "It's about the truth."

When he said that, I knew immediately it was, in fact, the key to the work we had accomplished. I willingly went down into all the parts of myself and my past that were hurtful, wounding, and painful, and I discovered the truth (as best I could) in each situation. Then, not only did I acknowledge the truth of what actually happened, but we took the time to bring about restoration with healing truth. Truth that could have been spoken. Truth that could have been lived. All of this brought healing to the past, which brought healing to my present.

Most people do not want healing. They are willing to settle for relief. Most people end their inner work after they reach the first flutters of liberation. *I'm all better*, they believe. But this is premature. Relief is simply the first layer. There is so much more. How much truth are you willing to wade through to come to complete healing? This is a longer and likely more painful process. So ask yourself, "Do I want *relief* or do I want *healing*?" For the deepest healing, truth is one of the main paths.

> Do I want *relief* or do I want *healing*?

Over the years I have learned to be able to look at myself in ways I never could before. I have grown accustomed to digging to unearth the deepest truth I can find. Bringing those places into the light, the presence of God, has been so freeing. But the process takes time. I had to walk into the shallow end of the pool and learn to make my way into the deep end. As I learned to tread water in the deep end, I found that my fears increasingly subsided. Instead of wanting to hide, I longed to dive deeper because freedom felt so good. Acknowledging weakness, brokenness, and wound-edness became the path to freedom and transformation.

At times, my counselor was surprised at my level of "Let's do this!" But I had reached a point where staying the way I was had become more unbearable than any wound I had to overcome or any truth I had to look squarely in the eye. The movement from denial to being willing to see the truth usually comes after the former way stops working. We sometimes seek truth only after the pain of hiding from it overwhelms us.

Dr. David Benner has said, "Any hope that you can know yourself without accepting the things about you that you wish were not true is an illusion. Reality must be embraced before it can be changed. Our knowing of ourselves will remain super-ficial until we are willing to accept ourselves as God accepts us—fully and unconditionally, just as we are." Benner also shares the following Thomas Merton quote: "There is no greater di-saster in the spiritual life than to be immersed in unreality, for life is maintained and nourished in us by our vital relation with reality." Benner goes on: "The truly spiritual life is not an escape from reality but a total commitment to it."[1]

Did you catch that? A truly spiritual life is a total commitment to reality. This is reality with a capital R that is engaged in truth with a capital *T*. Finding the truth, acknowledging it, and coming to terms with it are essential on the path to inner peace and freedom. What is the deepest truth you have access to in your current belief or situation? What kingdom realities can you draw on in this moment? Facing the truth is good and fruitful, no matter what our fears claim. This can be a challenge because of our tendency to self-protect. There is a version of me that doesn't want to stare truth in the face. It puts up walls and denials, and it will distract itself so that I won't go down into the deep well of truth. We must remember that on the other side of the truth is freedom, healing, and transformation. Because of this it can be helpful to begin to take small steps that prepare you to see the truth in any given situation.

For me that means beginning to notice and accept what I am doing. The strain of pushing against what is actually happening can be overwhelming. The first step toward peace is learning to accept what is. Notice I didn't say, *condone* what is; I said, *accept* what is. We must become people who acknowledge what is actually going on. If we don't do that, we run the risk of sinking into denial or entering into a string of unmet expectations. Both of these can easily lead to depression and do not lead us toward truth. We must grow accustomed to wearing our big kid pants and be willing to look at things as they are. Only then can we discern what is happening and make appropriate decisions for ourselves.

TRUTH AS KINGDOM REALITY

When it comes to truth and the way of transformation, it is helpful to remember that truth is not just about things we believe about God: theological orthodoxy, statements of faith, and doctrinal affirmations. Truth speaks even deeper than these to reality—kingdom reality and divine reality. This is the reality that Jesus came to live and reveal to us. Truth is how things are, not how they could be or should be or might be. Truth is how things *actually* are. Dallas Willard said more than once that "reality is what you bump into when you are wrong." That's a transforming vision of truth.

Here's an example: in our world, it is a commonly held assumption that our lives are all about having more possessions. Jesus, on the other hand, says that our lives do *not* consist in the abundance of our possessions (Luke 12:15). Who's right? Who has the best information? Who is dealing with reality? In which direction does true transformation lie? What is true here?

The invitation to transformation is learning to live in the truth. This is not merely an invitation to do more Bible studies and learn more biblical facts. It is an invitation to live into the kingdom and for my soul to become at home there. We can remind ourselves:

- I really do have a good Shepherd, who satisfies my every need.

- I really do have a faithful and affirming Father and thus I don't have to go around trying to prove my worth.

- I really do have an elder brother in Jesus who I can admire and brag about.

The transforming journey is about learning to align ourselves with Jesus, becoming accustomed to and living with assumptions rooted in divine reality. This is the reality Jesus embodies and proclaims. He models for us a life lived in keeping with God's kingdom realities. Jesus is the most real person who has ever lived. Being real isn't just about following every impulse that arises from within us. Jesus is the One who came and lived a true and real life. Might that not be part of his meaning when he says, "I *am* the truth"?

Now, Jesus often found himself in conflict with the Jewish leaders of his time. Their agenda was not the same as his. He had come to announce the kingdom *of* God. They seemed bent on protecting their own religious kingdoms *for* God. Theirs seemed to be anything but a strategy for actual transformation. Jesus said to the Pharisees that they searched the Scriptures daily because they believed that in them they had life, but that those very Scriptures testified about him (John 5:39). There is a difference between truth *about* and truth *in*. Our relationship with Jesus draws us into truth—into reality.

We can't think of anyone who identifies the Pharisees as their heroes of faith. But, in our most honest moments, we have to admit to there being a bit of a Pharisee in each of us. We don't like admitting it, but it's true. We're not necessarily talking about their legalistic religion, but about their tendency to focus on outward things instead of inner realities.

Jesus' words about these leaders in Matthew 23 are helpful. While we sometimes wish we could read those words as applying to others, it's better to take them to heart in ways we need to hear them. For example, Jesus says to a listening crowd, "The teachers of the law and the Pharisees sit in Moses' seat. So you must be careful to do everything they tell you. But do not do what they do, for they do not practice what they preach" (Matthew 23:2-3). It is possible to have a position of authority without a life of credibility. It is possible to proclaim a message rooted in Scripture without a life rooted in Scripture. At times we have found ourselves there. We have had right answers without a good life. It is possible to teach something that we have not yet been transformed by. When we do this, we weaken our influence by living in a way that is not in harmony with what we teach.

Most of us would like to be a good influence in our circles. As such, we are not only invited to practice *what* we preach, but to practice *before* we preach. We speak with credibility when we speak from the lived experience of transformation. When we want to share something from the Scriptures with another, we would do well to first reflect personally on the passage in focus. What is God saying about how we might change and enter into the gift of transforming grace this passage extends to me? When we live this way, we find that we are able

> What is God saying about how we might change and enter into the gift of transforming grace?

to share a lived and living word with others and not just a technically accurate word of truth.

Influence is not primarily about right answers as much as it is about a transformed life that speaks. We don't want to find ourselves speaking words of good news from a life that is more bad news. We want our lives to recommend our message. Paul says to Timothy, "Watch your life and doctrine closely" (1 Timothy 4:16). The invitation is not only to get doctrine right but to live whole and holy.

Jesus said of some of the Jewish leaders: "They tie up heavy, cumbersome loads and put them on other people's shoulders, but they themselves are not willing to lift a finger to move them" (Matthew 23:4). He was saying that there is a way of interacting with others that doesn't help. There is a way of communicating right answers in a burdensome manner without offering any help in carrying those burdens. A load of "shoulds," "ought tos," and "need tos" is offered without much "how to" or "let me help." This is not the way of Jesus.

In this way, spiritual influence can even become abusive. When someone doesn't experience the challenges of growing in Christ in their own life, it becomes easy for them to load others up with unbearable burdens they aren't trying to bear themselves. But when we live into the transforming invitation of Jesus, we can empathize with the struggles of spiritual growth and will be less likely to burden others with unreasonable and unrealistic expectations.

One of our mentors once said that too much preaching sounded to him like some variation on the theme of "Do better and do more." Here's how to be a better neighbor, a better husband, a better friend, a better parent, a better Christian. We are told what all this should look like without being given much power or help to actually live it. Good teaching doesn't just tell people what they should be doing; it shares how they might live in fruitful and transforming relationship with God, one another, and the world around them.

There is one more description of these leaders that we've needed to be attentive to: "Everything they do is done for people to see" (Matthew 23:5). Focusing on what others think about us does not lead to transformation. It is not transforming to become a master of appearance management. People may be fooled, but reality is still reality. It's too easy to settle for appearing transformed rather than actually *being* transformed.

Jesus unpacks the appearance management of some of the Jewish leaders by talking about their very noticeable "phylacteries." These were small boxes containing key Scriptures that were worn on the forehead or hand. Though meant as a reminder that what God says is real, these people were wearing them to look especially spiritual to others.

What are some of our own modern-day phylacteries? What do we put on to impress others with our holiness or devotion? Is it a particular tone of voice we use when praying? Is it the kind of book we carry around or quote from? Is it false humility in response to words of appreciation or affirmation? Is it using the right vocabulary or attending the right events? Is it making sure others know about our praying or giving or other spiritual practices?

The Jewish leaders Jesus was talking about practiced spiritual authority to maximize publicity. Instead of seeking to cultivate beauty of soul, they learned how to put on the right face and the right posture to impress as many people as possible. Today, they would love standing behind a microphone but wouldn't be very interested in serving behind the scenes.

We live in the place of transformation when we focus on the reality of who God is and respond with a willingness to change in response. We avoid the place of transformation when we focus instead of what others think of us, whether they like us or honor us.

Jesus highlights the tendency these leaders had to put their confidence in titles like rabbi, father, and teacher. Alan has been "pastor" most of his adult life. It has been important for him to remember that he is a pastor underneath the great Pastor, rather than behaving as though he has primary authority in anyone's life. His authority is not about titles but about his life. The graced authority of true transformation is potent and secure.

Seeking to impress others gets in the way of true transformation because it focuses on what things look like to others rather than on the substance of what actually *is*. However, we may find it hard to be patient with the kind of lifting up that humility leads to because it can take longer than the kind of lifting up we do for ourselves. For example, we felt that God gave us some promises about expanding our influence and the scope of our work back in the early years of our ministry. We looked for how to make this happen. Looking back, God wasn't giving us a self-promotion assignment. God was promising that he was going to work in us in such a way that we might be able to be trusted with broader opportunities to serve. But while we were expecting that process to take months, it actually took decades.

The God who lifts us up through deep inner transformation is patient in his work, even if we aren't. God makes promises to Abraham that take twenty-five years to be realized. Moses waits forty years in the desert in apparent obscurity before he comes to the burning bush. Joseph's dream takes at least a dozen or more years to even begin to be realized, and more than that before his family witnesses the reality of his dreams. Transformation takes time, but it is time spent building something of real, lasting good.

What is the price of non-transformation? We see it in a potent word Jesus uses to describe these Jewish leaders: *woe*. Woe is the opposite of blessed. Many of the woes of my (Alan's) life are troubles I've brought on myself. (Not all, but many.) I've settled for empty admiration rather than seeking true blessing. I've wanted the crowd to praise how I come across without simply and humbly seeking the real favor of the Father. Appearance management has never been a blessed way of life for me. Repentance has. Repentance is the good news that real transformation is available, possible, and desirable.

> **What is the price of non-transformation?**

Listen to how Jesus unpacks the woeful way of non-transformation. He points out that some claimed to be God's faithful children but lived lives out of tune with the Father. They rejected the life of God right in front of them in Jesus and, in doing so, closed the door to everyone who was following their leadership. Their outward-focused, appearance management approach to religious life ended up shutting the door to the kingdom in the faces of the men and women they were leading. They didn't humble themselves under the actual kingship of God. They preferred to have the devotion of the people rather than seeking actual devotion to God.

An orientation toward inner transformation focuses not on ourselves, but away from ourselves and on the King. We enter deeply into a real kingdom for ourselves and then, from that place of being at home in the kingdom, we serve as many as will join us here. Faith is dealing in heavenly realities that will transform us as we encounter them.

It's a woeful life when we are more committed to others joining our movement than inviting them into a transforming journey with Jesus. Some are tempted to convert others to their own perspectives, understandings, or opinions rather than inviting them to turn to God. This kind of passionate evangelism distorts the lives of others rather than transforming them. There is a great difference between inviting people to the person of God and inviting them into a belief system about that God. One produces transformed souls. The other produces clones. What a woeful thing this is.

Instead, an orientation to transformation invites others to trust and follow the God we've come to trust and follow. We aren't winning them to ourselves. We are pointing them to Jesus. Jesus then transforms our lives together in community. We make every effort to become a son or daughter of the kingdom in a way that recommends this way of life to all who witness it.

It's a woeful life when we resort to oaths and promises to prove the truthfulness of our words and our lives. It is woeful to want to appear trustworthy rather than simply becoming trustworthy. This is how empty religion comes about. The realities of God are forgotten in favor of empty words. The Jewish leaders focused on financial resources over worship (temple versus gold of the temple), human offerings over divine presence (altar versus the gift on the altar). It is always tempting to focus on things *about* God rather than on God himself.

Participating in religious activity without engagement with the living God creates a great deal of misery. When the Christian life becomes all about things like Bible studies, church services, regular giving, and missions trips, but forgets that God is real and alive in the midst of them, we are on the woeful path of non-transformation.

A transformation orientation remains awake to the reality of God in the midst of everything we do. Every single spiritual practice, in solitude and in community, engages with the presence of God with us in Christ. Every ministry task, every mission effort, every good work is just one more way to walk with Jesus on his transforming way.

It is a woeful life when we are scrupulous with minutiae and careless with what is precious and priceless. Some Jewish leaders had the bad habit of being obsessed with little observances and neglectful of what mattered most. They scrupulously measured their spices to give their ten percent to the temple, but they utterly failed to live just, merciful, and faithful lives. They could go to church without fail and never get any church into their lives. This is empty and heart-breaking. When our orientation is only on appearances, we may become riveted to miniscule righteousness at the expense of actually loving what is right.

An orientation to transformation learns to keep first things first, remembers what matters most, and always makes this the focus—the engine—of our life and work. Transformation occurs as we learn to keep our eyes on what is central to the life of God and let the peripheral remain on the periphery where it belongs. *It is a woeful life when we settle for appearing holy rather than becoming holy.* Jesus used the image of polishing the outside of the cup while failing to clean the inside. Trying to look good and right when others are looking but not becoming that person on the inside creates a great deal of stress. Looking good on the outside without becoming good inside is not a happy thing. Jesus urged us to "make the tree good." They were satisfied to make the tree *look* good.

Instead, an orientation to transformation focuses on what is happening in our hearts—our inner person—which is where transformation actually occurs. Then, we have freedom and per-spective to show the way of transformation to others. When internally we have become dirty with greed, lust, or any number of other forms of selfishness, we don't pretend otherwise by putting on a clean, nice face. We welcome the transforming presence of God to shine within us. If you were eating soup from a bowl and you could choose only one side of the bowl to be sure was clean, would you choose the inside or the outside? Dumb question, right? That's Jesus' point!

It's a woeful life when we put on an outward appearance of being alive in faith when we feel dead inside. Grace enlivens us and transforms us internally. This produces an actual likeness to

God in us. It's unfortunate whenever Christian leadership focuses on creating the appearance of godliness without the substance to support that appearance. We pretend, hoping that someday our true lives will look something like our act. Appearance management has a way of preventing the transforming touch of grace on our inner realities. The faults and shortcomings we hide only go deeper over time.

An orientation to transformation cultivates the vital presence of God within us (which will bear the fruit of righteousness), rather than spending so much energy putting on a show of holiness. There are few processes more important in transformation than our lives becoming more alive in the kingdom of God. Ironically, when we talk about leaders who "fall from grace" (by which we tend to mean a fall from public favor), we might actually be witnessing a moment when they fall *into* grace.

Jesus famously says that "the truth will set you free" (John 8:32). But that line often gets wrenched from the story in which it is found. Jesus first says to his Jewish friends who had come to trust in him, "If you hold to my teaching, you are really my disciples. *Then* you will know the truth, and the truth will set you free" (John 8:31-32). Some read this as a statement about theology and right doctrines. As far as this goes, we haven't a problem. But we prefer to think in terms of kingdom reality.

Jesus isn't saying, "You being right and others being wrong will set you free," or "Arguing your theological system will set you free." He invites these Jewish followers to trust and live into everything they are learning from Jesus. He is talking about the realities of God's kingdom. If they live into these truths, they'll discover the freedom that is the atmosphere of this good kingdom Jesus has come to announce and proclaim.

The truth Jesus is talking about is personal. It is relational. And believing the truth is a matter of allegiance to the person of Jesus in loving and obedient friendship. This is the place of freedom. This is the place of transformation.

A REFRESHED VISION

In *An Unhurried Leader,* Alan shared an eight-stage vision of spiritual leadership that we experienced in prayer many years ago.[2] It began with the image of a tree becoming rooted, moved on to people eating from the tree, and then culminated in trees growing, row by row, across the United States. It was the representation of us growing solid roots, mentoring others in the same, then leading to more fruitfulness and expansion.

As we began to move into and build Unhurried Living, I (Gem) found myself revving in all the wrong ways for the first six months. We both stepped out of one non-profit and into one that we began on our own, with no safety net of any kind. You can imagine the fears I was feeling in the middle of that transition. My anxiety was high, and I am embarrassed to say that it was a major engine for our first six months.

But after those six months, I could feel my creative and physical energy coming to a screeching halt. I had managed to get us set up with some of our content and infrastructure, but the excitement of new beginnings was wearing off, and all I was left with was my anxiety. It was no longer working. This "inner brake" that I experienced was a sheer gift of God. My heart of hearts did not want to operate from anxiety but from grace, peace, and an overflowing soul. Something had to change.

So, one day as I was pondering the end of my anxiety engine and hoping for a more peaceful one, I approached Alan and said,

"My anxiety-filled way isn't working. I need a fresh vision. Remember that old eight-stage vision from so long ago? I think I need a refreshed version of it. Can we pray like we did back then and see if God will enliven it for us?" Alan heartily agreed. We prayed and God did, indeed, enliven it for us.

As we prayed, we brought back to mind one of the final images in the eight-stage vision of the multitude of trees spanning across the United States. As Alan prayed out loud, I began to see in my mind an image of a grey, circular well overlaid onto the tree-covered US map. The well was made of stacked stones, and water was spilling out over the edges. Jesus was sitting next to the well, and he offered me a drink. It brought to mind the story of the woman at the well to whom Jesus said, "Everyone who drinks this water will be thirsty again, but whoever drinks the water I give them will never thirst. Indeed, the water I give them will become in them a spring of water welling up to eternal life" (John 4:13-14).

The image shifted, and I was transported to invitational language found in Ephesians 2:4-10:

> But because of his great love for us, God, who is rich in mercy, made us alive with Christ even when we were dead in transgressions—it is by grace you have been saved. And God raised us up with Christ and seated us with him in the heavenly realms in Christ Jesus, in order that in the coming ages he might show the incomparable riches of his grace, expressed in his kindness to us in Christ Jesus. For it is by grace you have been saved, through faith—and this is not from yourselves, it is the gift of God—not by works, so that no one can boast. For we are God's handiwork, created in

Christ Jesus to do good works, which God prepared in advance for us to do.

Remembering myself as seated with Christ in the heavenly realms, I was reminded to "serve from *this* place." I imagined myself leaning in to Jesus for counsel, to listen and learn. I was being invited to live, lead, and serve from a peaceful, relational connection. This was the truth of the situation. Not my anxiety. I did not have to drive or push Unhurried Living somewhere. Jesus was inviting me into a refreshed vision of spiritual leadership. I could receive refreshment and counsel from him and remember that I move from a place of grace. The good work I do has been prepared by a loving trinitarian community, and I have been invited into that community. I can heartily serve from such a place.

ENGAGING TRANSFORMATION

This vision illustrates another important triad of formational dynamics that follows *open, aware, and willing* shared earlier.[3] This second triad is *invitation, intention,* and *response.* We can live into the truth of our situation by taking discerning action that is rooted in relationship and grace.

Invitation: What is God's invitation to you? Once I stopped hitting my thumb with the hammer of anxiety, I was able to welcome the invitation for a vision of a new way forward. Invitations are so much nicer than "to dos," which sometimes feel more demanding or disconnected from communion with God. As Jesus met me in the image, his extended hand and leaning in were pure invitations to engage relationally. And my heart responded easily to that invitation.

Intention: What is the yes you want to say? My intention flowed directly from Jesus' gracious invitation to "lead from this place." Intentions are the yeses we want to say, connecting mind and heart. My yes was to move forward with the image of being in constant consultation with my good Shepherd, the One who quenches all of my thirsts. This easily became my intention and keeps me steady even now.

Response: How do you want to proceed? Intention then moves beautifully into response. Responding is answering the question "How do I want to proceed?" For me, that meant acknowledging that I was not a slave to the anxiety and fear that had been driving me for those first few months. My response was to engage from a place of simple trust in the One who is with me. When I catch myself falling back into anxiety, I can now draw on this process as often as I want. I make my way back to trust in the truth of God's great love and my aliveness in Christ.

WHY ASK WHY

Ricardo Semler offers a fascinating TED talk titled "How to Run a Company with (Almost) No Rules."[4] Near the end of his talk, Semler mentions the idea of asking three whys in a row when looking for wisdom in a situation. He moves through this idea quickly, barely touching on it and not unpacking the idea fully. But it seems to be a tool with potential for finding deeper truth about ourselves or a particular situation. Semler says of the three whys: The first why is usually fairly easy to answer. The second why is a little more difficult to see. The third why causes you to look even deeper into the situation. At this point you are nearing the center of why you are doing what you are doing.

Since Semler didn't really go into detail, I (Gem) decided to give it a try to see if it would work. For example, I'll begin with a statement: I am uncomfortable speaking in front of people. I notice this tendency in my life and want to get underneath it with truth so that I can move forward. Although I am uncomfortable with public speaking, it is a part of my job and I actually do want to share what I know. But the discomfort leads to anxiety, which leads to a number of other dynamics I'd rather not experience. So, let's go digging for deeper undercurrents of truth.

Here's the Q and A with three whys that would follow:

Statement: "I am uncomfortable speaking in front of people."

Why #1: Why are you uncomfortable speaking in front of people?

A: I'm afraid I'll forget what I'm saying, and I'll look like a fool in front of the audience.

Why #2: Why are you afraid of what people think?

A: I want people to think only well of me. I couldn't stand it if people had a negative experience of me.

Why #3: "I couldn't stand it" is fairly strong language. Why is it so important that people think only well of you?

A: My vision of myself is tied to how others perceive me. (Yikes. Did I just admit that?)

Okay, now we have something to work with. See how the first answer was relatively benign? I talked about forgetting stuff and looking like a fool. By the time I got to the third question, I was admitting the truth that I have an unhealthy connection to other people's perceptions of me.

At this point, I could look at my answer in depth. I could dialogue with myself and with God in prayer. Another flow of questions might emerge from this. My life becomes precarious if my view of myself is tied to the whims of others. Am I so flimsy that I cannot stand up against the opinions of other voices? If so, then I have some work to do. You can see that answering the third question doesn't solve the problem. It merely points more succinctly to where you need to focus some energy for growth or inner healing. It's about sinking deeper into truth.

I tried this with Alan to see if it would work for him. He decided upon a pressing issue in his life and started with a single why question. This process was so effective that by the time he got to the third why question he exclaimed, "Ouch!" He was able to get to the core of an issue that quickly. It sent him off into a meaningful time of processing and journaling.

Now, it may take more than three answers to get to your "ouch." But the point is to keep asking questions until you arrive at a deeper fear or an area of control. Once you've hit either one of those nerves, you are getting to the truth and the center of your situation.

Let's circle back to what my counselor said: "It's about the truth." When I pressed for further description, he said, "It's all about the truth. You meet somebody up at the truth. You ask a penetrating question, hopefully directed by the Holy Spirit. Then you let the person live with the question and answer it themselves. The lie gets untwisted and the truth sets them free."[5]

EXERCISE

Try out the three whys yourself. Begin with a statement. Then turn that statement into a question for the first why. Proceed from there by asking why two or more times. Refer back to the illustration above if you need more guidance. Don't be afraid of what you will find. Seeing, acknowledging, and being honest about what is actually happening are doorways on the path of transformation.

We can grow accustomed to desiring the deepest level of truth we can ascertain. You want more than relief. You want healing. That means that anything that you learn about yourself is good news. It means you can begin afresh in a new direction, along the path of truth.

BE TRANSFORMED

1. Bring to mind a situation in which you feel stuck. What would it look like to go on a search for the deeper truth?

2. In what ways might you be settling for relief instead of healing?

3. What are some steps you could take to go to the next level of healing?

4. How are you being transformed by what you know and proclaim?

6

PAIN

HOW ARE YOU SUFFERING?

Acceptance—*Acceptance goes hand in hand with letting go. This can be another difficult concept to deal with. However, it leads to great peace. Acceptance is not about resignation. Acceptance is gentler and kinder than resignation. It is not a giving up in a hopeless way, and it is not condoning anything. It is acknowledging what is and accepting it as such. Acceptance is the most holy version of "It is what it is." Lack of acceptance of what is actually happening holds many people back from the transformation they seek. You have to know where you are starting, where you actually are. Notice it, accept it, and keep moving.*

WHILE LEANING OVER MY BED pulling up the sheets one day, I (Gem) felt a small pop in my lower back. It wasn't too bad, just uncomfortable enough to be noticeable. Unfortunately, over the next two weeks the pain increased exponentially until I was lying in bed moaning in response to the relentless, throbbing pulse that shot down my entire left leg. I had no idea that kind of pain existed. I had recovered from three cesareans in giving birth to my sons, so I was familiar with pain. However, nerve pain is its own animal and is on a completely different level. After some testing, I was finally diagnosed as having a disc extrusion, and I began the long, slow process of disc decompression.

Very early on, before my diagnosis, Alan was driving me to the doctor for an MRI. I was laying in the back seat of our van listening to loud worship music through my earbuds. It was all I could do to pray and try to distract myself from the pain. I was listening to a song titled "Everything" by Tim Hughes. The chorus contained this beautiful repetition toward God: "Be my everything, be my everything, be my everything, be my everything."[1] Suddenly, in the midst of that melody, I had a moment of experiencing the presence of God like no other time in my life. There were no words, there was no vision, I simply knew in the deepest part of my being that God was with me. I had never experienced God's presence in this way before because I had never been in that much pain before. Without a doubt, God was letting me know he was with me *in* my pain.

That memory in the back of my van is forever etched in my soul. I know exactly how I felt—not the pain, but the presence. The *knowing*, God's with-ness, was undeniable. It is the grace of God that I cannot bring to mind the felt pain from that moment. I remember that it was unbearable, but I cannot feel it in my memory. But the sense of God with me? If I close my eyes, I am transported to the back seat of the van, and I easily re-enter that felt sense of *with*.

Words fail to describe this experience. I am trying my best, and the words I am choosing are as close as I can come, but the reality I experienced in my person is indescribable. Would I ever choose such pain? Never! But I wouldn't trade that experience of God's presence for anything. My sense of belief becoming an ever-deeper knowing is beyond a gift. I have been marked for life.

It was also during this time that I had the chance to receive love from Alan in a way I never had before. For a solid month he literally did everything. I did not see my kitchen for thirty straight days. I had only enough energy to get down the stairs, into the van, and over to my doctor appointments. That was it. When he wasn't caring for the boys or the house or working, he was sitting with me in a darkened room while I suffered. When spiking pain erupted in the middle of the night he would help me with my carefully scheduled pain medication and then read psalms out loud. It was all he could do to pray, and it was so necessary. I knew I was the focus of his attention, and it pierced through my pain as sheer presence.

The following year, even as the trauma of the nerves in my back was still quieting, I would begin to sink into a dark night of the soul. I was deep into mid-life, and I was taking another walk around the block of "things don't work the way they used to." Most of my inner constructs were crumbling at a new level, and I had no words.

Yet even in this sense of absence, I knew in my depths that God was there and would hold me. God could handle my not knowing, and he was patient and loving enough for me to work it through in my own way. Because of God's presence in my previous physical pain, I knew in my gut that he was present in my dark night. This was another divine breathing. God made his presence known in my physical pain. He then used that to provide a deeper level of faith to hold me when my soul was in pain and I was in the dark.

According to Frederick Buechner, "When someone we love suffers, we suffer with that person, and we would not have it otherwise, because the suffering and the love are one, just as it is with God's love for us."[2] If you are in a time of pain right now, I am so sorry for how this season feels. In no way do I want to minimize it or make it seem like it should pass quickly so you can get on with your life, even though that is likely exactly what you wish for. In the middle of your pain, it is good to remember that these kinds of experiences can lead us ever deeper into God's love. Pain and love can merge together as we lean into who God is, and his presence *with* us, in the midst of our actual circumstances.

THE THREE QUESTIONS

When I was still in the midst of suffering from my nerve pain I journaled three questions. I knew the answers were being formed in me and the process was ongoing. Even if I would have had the answers, I did not have the energy or coherence to formulate them or write them down. The answers were beyond words. In that process, the forming of the answers happened *in* me, deeper than my cognitive awareness. These may be three of life's deepest questions:

1. Is a person valuable when they aren't accomplishing anything?

2. Is God there if you can't feel him?

3. What is love?

As I write this, it has been almost exactly ten years since that summer of pain. I still don't know if I can answer these questions using words, but I'm going to try here. Julian of Norwich received sixteen revelations, or "Showings," of God's love that she experienced in her painful solitude with him. In no way do I compare what I share here with her "Showings." But I'm willing to call what follows in the next few paragraphs some of my "knowings" that emerged after my season of suffering in pain.

Is a person valuable when they aren't accomplishing anything? I'm cutting straight to the chase. The short answer is yes, of course, a person is valuable when they aren't accomplishing anything! Imagine a tiny infant who sleeps most of the time and can barely hold her head up because her neck muscles are still strengthening. To a new parent, there is hardly a more beautiful sight. Peach fuzz hair, perfect skin, and a forehead that smells like cookies. But what is she accomplishing? On any scale of productivity, nothing. But on the scale of being human, she is overwhelmingly valuable. She is valuable because she exists.

When you are suffering, how much you produce nearly always decreases somehow. In my case, I was completely unproductive. As I mentioned above, all I could do for a time was lay in bed and moan. A fruit of that time was an unchosen slowness. I was slower than slow. Everything came to a screeching halt. I didn't answer email. I didn't talk on the phone. I did no work. I walked at the achingly slow pace of an elderly and feeble person.

After the intense pain began to lessen, I realized I was left with a profound slowness within. My usual internal revving was gone, and the pace of my heart was quiet and steady. I remember being afraid of losing that inner pace as I began to re-engage the activities of my life. I didn't want to lose that holy slowness. I was

aware that an inner slowness could be a defining mark of a
mindfully present person in an extremely hurried and busy
culture. People need presence. And presence can only happen
when a person chooses or gives way to a slowed inner pace.

I discovered that my value was never at risk. Like that tiny
infant, I got to see that I was loved and valued by God simply
because I existed. And the extra added bonus is that God left me
with a new understanding of presence that I would be able to
offer to others. How valuable is it for someone to be present with
you? The value is incalculable.

Is God there if you can't feel him? Another fruit of that time
was that I was left with a new sense of the "eternalness" of God.
Time stood still for me, and, in that season, clock time began to
lose its meaning. I mentioned that in that moment when God
met me in the back of the van, I had a distinct sense of God's
presence. Yes, it lasted just a moment, and, yes, it marked me for
life. At the same time, for most of that season of pain I had no
sense of God. I was deep in my pain and could not wait for it to
be over. The sense of God's with-ness was deeper than a feeling,
deeper than cognition.

God is not bound by my timeline or even by my senses. He is
boundless, eternal, everywhere present, and "every time" present.
We are back to the knowing. It is a deeper sense of presence and
trust than the surface feeling. Those of you who have experienced God in this way know exactly what I am talking about. It
is a grace that is indescribable. So, yes, God is there, even if I
can't feel him.

What is love? I had read and learned from Mother Teresa that,
when in pain, it can be helpful to look to the suffering and crucifixion of Christ. A few times, when I was in the most severe

pain, I prayed, "Jesus, how did you do this?! My pain is only a fraction of the suffering of the cross, so I cannot imagine the pain you suffered. The excruciating beatings, the humiliation, the nails, the physical torture of the crucifixion. How did you choose to do this?" I could not fathom a love that would choose such pain and sacrifice. Feeling my own pain led me to the pain of the cross, and there I found love. Unending, sacrificial love from a Savior who knows pain and suffering. And he joined me in mine. That is love.

I offer these questions to you as you sit in your own pain. You don't need to resonate with my answers or even try to formulate your own. It is okay to let God meet you in the questions themselves.

NUMBING THE PAIN

I (Alan) have had a bad habit of avoiding or numbing my pain. I pretend I'm not in pain. It doesn't matter much if it is severe pain or mild discomfort. I'm probably not the only person with this issue. Pretending we don't hurt—trying to avoid or numb pain—does not let it do its work. Pain is communication that something is out of alignment. I may or may not have the power to re-align whatever that might be, but I can at least listen to whatever message pain might be offering me. There might be wisdom for my way forward in it.

> Pain is communication that something is out of alignment.

My tendency to avoid or numb pain is an addictive instinct. Recovery comes as I learn to experience my pain, face my pain, even live my pain. When I've done this, I've discovered it to be a path of transformation.

As a practical example, I've had quite a bit of lower back pain as I move into later middle age. If I listen to it, I realize two things. I'm carrying more weight in my belly than I need to. And my hamstring muscles are tighter than they need to be. So, losing a little weight and practicing hamstring stretches could help reduce the pain. In this way, I'd be listening to pain for the purpose of transformation.

But sometimes I prefer ignoring the pain or just bearing with it. If I feel pain but opt to numb, medicate, escape, even divert myself from engaging pain as an opportunity—a doorway—to holy transformation, I might be choosing empty relief over authentic change.

I can practice giving attention to pain in my body, in my emotions, in my thoughts, in my soul, and then listening for what that pain might be seeking to say to me. What is out of order in me? What is misaligned? What is broken? What is empty? And then, how might God wish to meet me as my Guide, my Counselor, my Healer, the One who fills my plate? Perhaps there is a way forward that relieves the pain. Perhaps I will find I must bear with pain. (I'm not claiming that all pain is as helpful a guide as this. There is such a thing as chronic pain, which is its own difficult place of encounter with God.)

There is wisdom in the Scriptures about how suffering and transformation are connected. It isn't the kind of wisdom that we've always welcomed, but it is good, life-giving counsel. For example, consider how James speaks to a church facing a great deal of hardship. They are having to persevere under countless trials. Some among them are lacking basic clothing and daily food. There was fighting and quarreling among them. James encourages them to find patience like the prophets and Job did in their suffering (James 1:2, 12; 2:15-16; 4:1; 5:7-11).

After his opening greeting, James has some rather stark counsel for these brothers and sisters: "Consider it pure joy, my brothers and sisters, whenever you face trials of many kinds" (James 1:2). If we were to suggest you write a list of ten things that give you pure joy, what would be on it? Would it be a child or a grandchild? A favorite vacation spot? A special restaurant? James suggests "trials of many kinds." For most of our lives, we'd have avoided putting that on our list. What is James talking about? Is he a masochist? And why would you start a letter this way?

Thankfully, James offers a reason for his counsel: "Because you know that the testing of your faith produces perseverance" (James 1:3). Trials, hardships, challenges all have a way of testing what we believe about ourselves, about God, and about reality. Pain has a way of dispelling fantasies and illusions. Perseverance is a priceless, precious quality. Don't we want to be able to stay with something important even when it's difficult, even in the face of failure, even when we experience opposition? Don't we want to have power not to give up when things are hard?

But James gives what strikes us as a deeper, more hopeful purpose in the trying experiences of our lives. He goes on to say that we can "let perseverance finish its work so that you may be mature and complete, not lacking anything" (James 1:4). Those last six words sound pretty inviting. We've prayed many times asking God to grow our trust in him or for him to make us whole in ways that we haven't been so far or to provide us something we're lacking. But we seem to always be surprised when we're brought to such places along a painful path of hardship. Perseverance leads to good and lasting work in us. If we let it, we'll discover that much of what we've longed for in our lives will be realized. That's been our experience.

When we dream about our journey with God, we dream of being people who are mature, who are whole, who enjoy truly good things. We don't know many people whose dream in life is to be immature, incomplete, and lacking much! No one has that kind of vision for their lives. But the path of this kind of transformation takes us through the many hard, even painful places each of us walks over a lifetime. We learn how to live these places in the Presence, rather than letting them become reasons for avoiding God's presence.

James has written to a suffering church. They're discouraged. They're struggling. They're wrestling. James is trying to encourage them that God will use all of this hard stuff. This is not meaningless suffering; it will produce fruit.

THE UNEXPECTED GIFT OF PERSEVERANCE

Perseverance is one of the virtues that develops in our growing relationship of surrender to God. Hard experiences invite us to entrust ourselves to God. Our endurance, our ability to stay with the hard places, enables us to grow in maturity, holiness, wholeness, and abundance.

James mentioned Job as an example to his friends in Christ. Think about Job's experience. As the book begins, he is a respected man, a good man, a wealthy man, a man with a great family. He's a someone who has everything he could wish for. But only twelve verses into this forty-two-chapter book, Job loses his wealth, his livelihood, and all of his children through enemy attacks and natural disasters (Job 1). Eventually, he loses physical health and his wife's support (Job 2:7-9). Job is the book in the Bible to which we can go when we are facing hardship of many kinds.

It doesn't help much to tell people who are in pain, "I read a great chapter about pain as a pathway to transformation. Lucky you!" Think about Job's friends. They are able to sit with him in empathetic silence for a week, but they finally grow tired of listening to Job's complaints and succumb to an impulse to explain Job's suffering or solve it (Job 2:13; 4:1-6). They say things like, "You know, Job, you must have done something bad to be suffering like this. Figure out what you did wrong to deserve all this."

When you read the counsel that Job's friends give him, they sound, in many ways, technically true. But Eugene Peterson, in his introduction to the book of Job in *The Message*, writes, "It is the 'technical' part that ruins them. They are answers without personal relationship, intellect without intimacy. The answers are slapped onto Job's ravaged life like labels on a specimen bottle. Job rages against this secularized wisdom that has lost touch with the living realities of God."[3]

Peterson further offers these priceless words: "The book of Job is not only a witness to the dignity of suffering and God's presence in our suffering but is also our primary biblical protest against religion that has been reduced to explanations or 'answers.'"[4] We welcome wise counsel from those who have been tempered by suffering. They don't offer easy answers or glib counsel, and we aspire to grow as this type of counselor to those God gives us to serve.

GLORIOUS SUFFERINGS?

Paul the apostle adds his voice of witness to James's and Job's about the unexpected gift of pain and perseverance. In his letter to the Romans, this is how he expresses it: "Not only so, but we also glory in our sufferings, because we know that suffering produces perseverance; perseverance, character; and character, hope. And hope does not put us to shame, because God's love has been poured out into our hearts through the Holy Spirit, who has been given to us" (Romans 5:3-5). We haven't always had as much vision as Paul does here, but we're grateful to learn from his experience.

Doesn't his language sound a bit foreign? Maybe you're like us in generally seeing suffering and pain as something always to be alleviated. That's at least our usual first impulse. It's certainly our usual response to pain of any kind. Yet Paul *glories* in his suffering. Is he a masochist like James, or are they both on to something good?

Paul surely doesn't enjoy suffering, but the suffering he faces as he follows Jesus in the power of the Holy Spirit is purposeful. The suffering Paul is talking about *produces* something. No woman relishes the great pain of labor. But there is grace and purpose in that pain as it brings with it the promise of a baby boy or girl. Football players probably don't enjoy the pain and suffering of a "hell week" at the beginning of summer training, but they like the freedom and strength it brings when the fall season begins.

Paul glories in all the sufferings that come as he follows Jesus and lives into his transforming purposes because of the good that comes through them. The process he describes is an organic one. Suffering is like soil in which something can grow. First of all, there's perseverance. He's echoing James' counsel here. This isn't just "put up with something because I haven't a choice." It's the ability to have staying power, lasting courage, gutsy endurance. Walking the path of transformation requires sustained perseverance. If the path gets hard and we give up, we won't experience much progress along the way.

This perseverance, when it becomes an established capacity in us, produces character. Character describes reliable capacities for sustained goodness and good work. It is the fruit of training and not mere trying. Hardship and trouble can be a kind of gym for our transforming souls if we'll let them. The temptation for us, though, has often been to avoid hardship or numb pain. The point isn't that we should hurt as much as possible. It is instead that hardship, trouble, and other pain are places to be with God and to recognize God with us.

Walking the path of transformation requires sustained perseverance.

Paul tells his friends in Philippi, "I want to know Christ and experience the mighty power that raised him from the dead. I want to suffer with him, sharing in his death, so that one way or another I will experience the resurrection from the dead!" (Philippians 3:10-11 NLT). Paul wants to be close to Jesus in every way possible. He wants to be part of Christ's glory, and he wants to be part of Christ's pain. This communion with Jesus in everything is a transforming power in Paul's life . . . and in ours.

As character like Christ's takes shape in us more and more, we find ourselves hopeful. We know God is with us in what is hard now. We grow confident that we will never be alone in anything hard on the path ahead. We really can do what is necessary because Christ is with us in it all. We envision the future as a path of great goodness that we'll enjoy and share with God and others no matter how challenging or painful certain stages of the journey might be. This isn't wishful thinking. It's the reality of empowering grace.

Hope like this, Paul says, "does not put us to shame" (Romans 5:5). Perhaps he's saying that hope that is the fruit of deep-rooted character is reliable. We won't find our hopes as mere wishful thinking or shallow optimism. We'll find great courage to hope with strengthening joy as we envision the path ahead.

ALL SHALL BE WELL

Don't get us wrong. We wish we were as joyful about tested faith as James and Paul seem to be. But we've learned that the hard things in life haven't managed to block God's purposes. He has been able to do what he wanted in and through our lives, even with those and even *through* those hard places.

But sometimes, we find ourselves wishing that transformation was as easy as many infomercials make weight loss sound, as easy as consuming some product or reading some book that would miraculously change us. But change usually involves at least a little discomfort.

Think of the well-known bit of classic spiritual wisdom "All shall be well." We're tempted to think that such a line came easily to the spiritual sage who coined it. It can sound nice and cozy. We've heard "all shall be well" used as a trite word of encouragement to someone who was suffering. But this kind of wellness did not arise from a recliner or a tropical resort.

Consider the life of Julian of Norwich, to whom God once spoke the words, "All shall be well, and all shall be well, and every manner of thing shall be well." Again, she doesn't write these words from an easy life in a wealthy fourteenth-century family. This bit of wisdom comes to her on her death bed in her thirties as she receives the gift of sixteen visions of Jesus. In one of those, she hears these words about all being well. Not only does she nearly lose her life from a serious illness (she lives another forty or so years after this), but she lives in the midst of one of the worst epidemics in world history, the Black Plague, in which tens of millions of people lost their lives. Her lifespan also came within the Hundred Years' War between England (her home country) and France during which millions died.[5] "All shall be well" were words that came to her in a life, a country, a world in which very little seemed well.

This wise spiritual woman came to these comforting insights in a place where her need for comfort seemed measureless. We all have moments of discomfort, pain, even what we might rightly call suffering. The opportunity in the midst of these almost inevitable places in our lives is to decide whether we might live into them with God, who is with us there. We might pray our pain with angry or grieving words, but the place of pain can become for us a place of learning the true wellness of soul available to us or the breadth of true wellness on our eternal horizon.

THE TUNNEL VISION OF PAIN

Pain, whether physical or not, leads to a kind of tunnel vision in which life becomes hemmed in with physical and emotional limits. The focus becomes asking, "How am I going to get through this day?" The world is smaller than it could be because the pain overshadows any broad view of life.

We witness this day-to-day brokenness at the gas station pump, the grocery store line, the school parking lot, or the freeway. There is so much anger, entitlement, and self-centeredness. In some cases, this is simply a sign that people are overwhelmed and they have had to resort to a kind of tunnel vision just to get through the day.

Presence is about seeing through the fog of their behavior to the person inside. The mom who just found out that her son takes drugs. The man who just found out his wife is cheating on him. The woman who just received news of breast cancer. The couple who just decided to get a divorce. This stuff is happening all around us. And people are trying to carry on amidst the weight of pain. Our job, as people of presence, is to see. We may not be able to help everyone, but we can help the one we are with. A kind word, a gentle smile, a listening ear, a quiet prayer.

Dallas Willard said that blessing is willing the good of another. In that moment, when you see a person acting out, you can step back, calm down, and take a moment to will good for that person. Let's be people who have eyes to see and ears to hear the cries of the hurting around us. Being present takes energy, and it is one of the greatest gifts we can give this busy, harried culture.

WOUNDED HEALER   *Slowness own Judgement*

Ann Morrow Lindbergh writes, "I do not believe that sheer suffering teaches. If suffering alone taught, all the world would be wise, since everyone suffers. To suffering must be added mourning, understanding, patience, love, openness, and the willingness to remain vulnerable."[6] The process about which Lindbergh speaks takes time. Each word she uses (*mourning, understanding, patience, love, openness, willingness*) is an unfolding. This process cannot be rushed, and each part is a deep work in and of itself. As we remain open to the love, guidance, and maturing process in which God has us, we can continue in this unfolding.

A few years ago we had a conversation with a young friend. She described a chronic physical issue in her body that was unresolved at that point. She shared the "advice" given by many well-meaning friends, advice that even included what God's will was in her situation. Most of it did not seem helpful to her soul.

In the midst of her suffering, the answers did not comfort. She was left holding questions, and they were indeed doing their work within her.

As we spoke, we didn't end up with any helpful solutions either. That was not the point of our conversation. But she did end up with the realization that her suffering kept her open to the Lord in new ways. She was given the gift of having a real-life way of relating to people who had unresolved issues in their own lives. She would decidedly not be handing out pat answers any longer. She would know how to sit with someone in their suffering. Her heart was open in new ways because of the chronic nature of her situation. We were so proud of this young woman as she made her way through her pain. She is going to be the kind of leader this next generation needs: authentic, vulnerable, loving. Unresolved pain is a wise teacher, if we will let it be so.

In *The Wounded Healer,* Henri Nouwen calls professional ministers to be willing to open themselves to others as fellow sufferers sharing their common pain and thereby finding healing. We are all ministers within our own spheres of influence. And it is from within our own places of pain and suffering that we become even more effective as we speak, live, and lead. People respond most deeply to lived grace.

Based on what we have discovered in our own lives, we have committed ourselves to listen to our friends and colleagues and to encourage them to remain open. Together we can mourn our losses and grow in understanding of one another. Together we can let patience and love grow into continued openness and vulnerability. Together we can discover how the reality of suffering keeps our hearts soft toward ourselves and

> People respond most deeply to lived grace.

toward others. Together we can allow our suffering to take us further into the depths of wisdom and maturity. Most people don't have a choice about whether or not they suffer. But we all have a choice about what we let take root in our heart as a result.

BE TRANSFORMED

1. Think back to a time of extreme pain. How did God meet you in the midst of it? How did grace show up in unexpected ways?

2. How do you typically numb your pain? As a famous TV doctor says, "How's that working out for you?"

3. Alongside knowing the power that raised Christ from the dead, what does it look like for you to suffer with Christ? How might this help you to experience resurrection in your life?

4. How can you extend grace to yourself or to your loved ones as you/they traverse pain?

7

FEAR

WHAT ARE YOU AFRAID OF?

handwritten:
- IRS
- Rejection
- Bad Health
- Family getting sick
- $ enough?

With—*My favorite way to use this word is with God. Or God with us. God, by his spirit, is within us. "You have searched me, LORD, and you know me. You know when I sit and when I rise; you perceive my thoughts from afar. You discern my going out and my lying down; you are familiar with all my ways" (Psalm 139:1–3). Using this word reminds me that I am not alone. Ever.*

IT WAS THE ERA OF THE HIPPIE, and I (Gem) was in elementary school. Woodstock had taken place just a few years earlier, and this particular summer a group of non-conforming young adults planned a gathering near our home in rural Washington. They had to drive past our property to get to their party location in the lush, tree-laden hills. I knew about this gathering because I heard my mom complaining about "those hippies." I

don't remember what she said, but I had a sense that hippies
were something to be avoided.

So that summer my cousin and I decided that we needed to
protect ourselves from those dangerous, free-spirited youth. We
determined to dig a hole in our front pasture as a kind of hippie
deterrent. If anyone decided to come toward our house, that
unsuspecting person would fall into our hole and break a leg,
rendering them unable to get to the house to harm us.

If either of us had been any kind of engineer, we would have
drawn up some plans for a hole deep enough for someone to fall
into and not climb out. However, in our youthful wisdom, we
decided to simply wing it. Armed with a single shovel and great
determination, we set out for the field to begin searching for the
perfect place to dig.

After carefully surveying the land, we found just the right
spot. It was about halfway up our driveway and just on our side
of the barbed wire fence that marked our property line. We were
sure that if hippies decided to climb through our fence, they
would choose this exact location. So we dug a hole that was
about one foot wide and about two feet deep, and we dubbed it
"The Hippie Hole." We were so proud! We had successfully protected ourselves against the flower children.

Over the course of my adult life, I have dug holes as well,
hoping that trouble would fall in and break its leg. As an adult,
my hole-digging has sometimes come in the form of my trying
to manage my fear—sometimes real, sometimes imagined, and
in a situation over which I actually had no control at all. Still, I
tried to manage the situation with my own shovel, hoping to
protect myself.

WHAT AM I AFRAID OF?

If we can answer the question "What am I afraid of?" we can more easily drill down toward the center of our issue. Multiple times I have found fear or anxiety underneath my anger, frustration, and perfectionistic tendencies.

Here is a very practical example. One time, when Alan and I were preparing to record a podcast, I found myself becoming very picky about the microphones and the sound of our voices on a test playback. I was edgy and snarky, and Alan and I found ourselves at odds with each other. A few minutes into a heated discussion about our sound quality, we caught ourselves and tried to turn the conversation in a more helpful direction.

As I thought about why I was so snippy, I realized that under it all was a fear of looking and sounding stupid. I was afraid of sharing what we were going to talk about that day, and it was coming out as judgment and perfectionism. As I shared my fears with Alan and acknowledged that they were real, I not only saw my fear, I *felt* my fear.

Feeling your fear is key to moving through it. We spend all kinds of misdirected energy trying to hide from, push away, or numb our fears. That's where we get into trouble as various addictions seek to keep our fears at bay. As I simply spoke aloud and then felt my fears, the angst of them began to dissipate and I became free. I could relax, and the stuff that I was worried about began to fade. Shining a light on my deeper fear brought calmness to the situation, and we were able to move forward. Fear can sometimes hide like that, masquerading as something else such as perfectionism or frustration. You then find yourself down a path that you didn't choose, and you can't figure out how you got there.

> Feeling your fear is key to moving through it.

This *speaking* out loud and *feeling* pattern can help at many levels of fear. Sometimes it's the mere acknowledgment that can take the sting out of your mood. However, sometimes it takes much more time and intention to notice, feel, and then move through fear. One of the reasons I was able to move through that podcast situation so quickly (besides the fact that it was not dire) was that I had already spent years practicing seeing things as they are, feeling my emotions, accepting what happened, and moving toward healing. No doubt, this can be a long process. We are talking about overcoming years of patterns of staying trapped in fear. On the path of transformation it is okay for things to take as long as they take. I encourage you to keep moving along the path, even if, at times, it feels as though you are wading through a vat of molasses.

Most of us have a built-in barrier to fear and will want to push it away at all costs. I encourage you to dig around a bit, find the fear, say it out loud, and let yourself feel it at the level in which you are able. As it is seen, the possibility for healing grows. Depending on the situation, the length of time you sit in the feeling will vary. And if you have deep-seated, overwhelming fears, it might be good to seek professional counsel. You don't need to traverse this path alone. In your day-to-day life, however, this process can be quite helpful for moving through situational fears. Remember that not feeling your fear is what leads to unhelpful behaviors because we then feel the need to numb ourselves to keep fear at bay.

GOD ALONE

On a lazy Saturday afternoon we were channel surfing on the TV, and Alan stopped briefly at an infomercial that was promoting a new kind of cooking machine that purported to be better than a stove top with gas or electric burners.

We both laughed out loud as the sales people told us that using a stovetop for the last fifty years of our lives has made us complete buffoons. The really smart people are using this new-fangled gadget that heats up food in this new-fangled way. Picture a woman standing in front of her disheveled pots and pans, lids everywhere, hair all messed up, and a "What do I do with all of this stuff?" look on her face.

Almost immediately, fear entered the mix. They proceeded to interview a fireman that told the story of his very first fire, which, of course, started on a stovetop. House fires are no laughing matter. But saying that this cooking machine could allay our fears and keep the house from burning down was a bit much.

Obviously, what we see in advertisements is meant to make us buy a product. Tapping into people's fears and manipulating their decisions is commonplace. Watch any informercial, and you will see at least one nod to fear. In fact, fear is a part of the formula advertisers use to get people to spend. That's how businesses make money. It takes a tremendous amount of effort to convince people to purchase something they do not need. And that force is exerted on each of us every day. Even if you don't watch much TV, ads scroll by on all of our social media. Because of this, we can subconsciously begin to believe that the solutions to our fears are found in some *thing* somewhere, that some *thing* will protect us and keep us safe—just like my "hippie hole."

The truth is that our souls can only find rest in *someone*. There is no other place to find true rest, peace, and freedom from fear.

Truly my soul finds rest in God;
    my salvation comes from him.
Truly he is my rock and my salvation;
    he is my fortress, I will never be shaken. (Psalm 62:1-2)

"I will never be shaken" is a statement about our fears. But I've often felt shaken, haven't you? When we experience the loss of a love one, we feel shaken. When we encounter financial challenges, we feel shaken. When we come upon life-altering decisions, we feel shaken. When we suffer extreme physical pain, we feel shaken. What does the psalm mean, "I will never be shaken"? Haven't we all felt shaken?

The word "truly" is used twice in this passage. It's as though David, the author, is convincing himself that what he is saying is true. "No, really. This is how it works," he seems to say. In another version, instead of the word "Truly" it says, "God only." Though these are different ways of phrasing, the meaning is clear. *For real, God is the only way my soul finds true rest.* So if there is actually something out there that provides the solutions to our fears, it isn't a gadget. It isn't a *thing*. It is God himself. God only.

> Oh, the freedom and love you can experience once you let yourself be exactly as you are in the presence of an all-knowing, all-present, generous, and loving God.

Over the years, as we've made our way through our own shaken experiences, we've learned that God meets us in those very moments. It is by making your way *through* your experience that the reality of not being shaken can grow in you. We wish there was an easier way. But with fear, the only way past it is through. And not just through, but *with* and through. Recalling the idea of feeling our fears, if you can remember that God is *with* you as you feel your fear, a whole new level of connection to God is available to you.

Sometimes we feel as though we cannot experience our negative feelings, like fear, in the presence of God. Somehow, we had to clean up before we could be together. But, oh, the freedom and love you can experience once you let yourself be exactly as you are in the presence of an all-knowing, all-present, generous, and loving God. If God is your fortress, then certainly he is with you as you make your way through your trying circumstances. Our deep desire here is to give you a vision for not letting fear be the boss of you. There is a way forward, and it is in the strong, loving presence of God. As we have taken risks in being exactly who we are in God's presence, which means bringing our fears along with us, we have found a loving and safe Father who sees and holds us even at our worst.

Another very practical way to work through fear is to remember that you have made it through every single moment and event in your life thus far. And you are still here. Every time we have spent days, weeks, or months worrying in anxiety or fear about some upcoming opportunity, we actually made it through. And most of those situations we have already forgotten. Whether it went well or not, it occurred, and we lived to tell about it (or forget about it). So why should we continue to waste any more time being afraid of things? When you find yourself standing at the precipice of a fearful experience, you can say to yourself, out loud, "I have made it through everything I have ever done in my life, even the worst of it. God was with me then, and he will be with me now."

A great prayer that springs from Psalm 62 is this: *My soul finds rest in God alone.* When you come across the next gadget that promises to quell your fears, try saying this prayer out loud. *My soul finds rest in God alone.* Our prayer for you is that your soul might take a deep breath, that you will find rest in God, and that he will allay your fears and anxieties.

AFRAID OFTEN

I (Alan) feel like I know a lot about fear because I've been afraid a lot. I mean *a lot*. I've felt afraid most of the way through writing this book. I've felt afraid often when I stand to speak or travel to train a group of leaders. I've felt afraid often throughout my life. Fear has often gotten in the way of my trying something that I believe God was inviting me to do. And I feel sad thinking back on that much fear.

But I've also often taken my fear with me into my life and work. I've said what I felt called to say or wrote what I believed I was supposed to write and others told me it helped. I wish I was less often fearful. Sometimes, I feel what John must have meant in his first letter when he says that there is no fear in love, and that perfect love casts out fear. When I've known and trusted in the love of God for me, I haven't been as afraid. When I've been living in love toward another, I haven't been as afraid either.

I needn't be afraid, but I am. God invites me to live increasingly free of fear, and sometimes I take him up on his invitation. But not always, and not as often as I might.

So of the eight questions this book focuses on, the one I've often found hardest has been this question about fear. I am an apprentice who has often needed to be reminded by the mentors in my life that I can work with energy and fire because of the gift of God's Spirit, which brings power, love, and self-discipline, and not the draining dynamic of timidity (see 2 Timothy 1:6-7).

Fear and anxiety are such a drain of energy if I listen to their threats, warnings, and dire predictions. I could, instead, listen to the voice of the One who seems always to be saying, "Alan, don't be afraid. You're not alone in this. I am with you." The thing is, the fears and anxieties that rise up in me are usually wrong. I mean, there are things that frighten me, but I'm talking about the fears that bubble up in my thoughts and emotions about imagined dark possibilities in my near future. I've imagined myself absolutely bombing in a speaking engagement. Surprisingly, that has never actually happened. I haven't always hit home runs in every engagement, but if I speak from my life and what I've learned from God along the way, it always seems to help.

In my experience as a spiritual director talking with many others, I find that fear just might be one of the hardest issues for many of us in our journey toward transformation. Perhaps that's why it also seems to be so common in the biblical narrative. Hundreds of times in the story of the Scriptures, God speaks the words "Do not be afraid." "Fear not" is a word God speaks to us when we face hardship, threat, or danger. And the most common promise God offers us in our places of fear is that *he will be with us.*

Remember God's words to Joshua as he prepared to enter the Promised Land:

> As I was with Moses, so I will be with you; I will never leave you nor forsake you. Be strong and courageous, because you will lead these people to inherit the land I swore to their ancestors to give them.
>
> Be strong and very courageous. Be careful to obey all the law my servant Moses gave you; do not turn from it to the right or to the left, that you may be successful wherever you go. Keep this Book of the Law always on your lips; meditate on it day and night, so that you may be careful to do everything written in it. Then you will be prosperous and successful. Have I not commanded you? Be strong and courageous. Do not be afraid; do not be discouraged, for the LORD your God will be with you wherever you go. (Joshua 1:5-9)

Three times God repeats a form of the words "Be strong and courageous." Often I make the mistake of thinking that courage means feeling no fear. Rather, in God's counsel to Joshua, courage is the ability to act in keeping with God's counsel in the face of fearful realities. I may feel strong fear and act with genuine courage. In fact, courage usually requires the presence of some fear. It doesn't take great courage to buy dinner at a fast food restaurant (well, it might take a little, depending on the restaurant!). It doesn't take courage to sit in my recliner and read a book. These do not provoke any fear. But sitting to do creative work of any kind always seems to require courage, at least for me, because it stirs within me fears of inadequacy, failure, or potential rejection. In such a place, God comes to me and encourages, "Be strong, Alan, and take courage. I am with you. I will be with you wherever you go and whatever you do."

God also invites Joshua to obedience. He invites Joshua to stay in the good and true place of his counsel. Obedience is not merely dutiful subservience to an arbitrary rule. It is loving allegiance to the true way of a good King. We obey so that we might stay in the place and on the path that is vital, fruitful, and beneficial. In his invitation to obedience, God isn't just saying, "Keep the rules." He is saying, "Live your life in and with me. Don't wander from me. Don't turn from me. Stay close. Let's walk together. Let's work together."

And so we meditate on the Scriptures to settle within ourselves a vision of this loving God and his ways. We come to assume God's kingdom as the "real world" in the midst of our human realities.

The command to be strong and courageous is one that Joshua would call to mind often. When he was in the battle for the

Promised Land and was marching with his whole army, God once again said to him, "Do not be afraid of them; I have given them into your hand. Not one of them will be able to withstand you" (Joshua 10:8).

While I have never actually gone to war with weapons and soldiers against a foreign army, I *am* in a battle with enemies like fear, self-doubt, insecurity, or anxiety. Here, God seems to say to me, "Alan, do not be afraid of your enemies. When you go up against them, they will fall into your hands. Nothing will stand against you." Forces like my own fear, anxiety, self-doubt, or insecurity would hinder me from entering in to all the good the Lord has for me. I'm sorry to say that this is a familiar struggle. I encounter fear like this just about every time I engage a new piece of my work in ministry. If I let it, fear would hinder me from taking even the first step. But my fears and anxieties have proven to be miserably poor predictors of the future.

I wonder what might have been going through Joshua's mind when he heard God speak these words of strength and courage. Might he have thought, as I do, *But I feel weak and fearful?* But isn't this just what the Lord would have been speaking to? If there is no fear, why speak courage? If there is no anxiety, why speak peace? If there is no weakness, why speak strength? Weakness, insecurity, anxiety, or fear are never the ultimate reality. God's strength, confidence, peace, and love are. Transformation is the process of coming to live in these kingdom realities.

Strength and courage are for action—God with me wherever I go (and, by extension, in whatever I do). Courage is acting in the face of my anxiety and fear. A counselor of mine once told me, "Take your fear and anxiety with you." Rather than be paralyzed by them, I take them along and take action. There is a

difference between acknowledging my fears and taking holy
action in the face of them. Action and progress quiet the voices
and answer the false arguments of
anxiety and fear.

> Courage is acting in the
> face of my anxiety and fear.

In the writings of one of my favorite historic spiritual directors,
Reginald Somerset Ward, comes this simple, potent insight
about our fears: "In considering fear, there is only one medicine
which can produce an absolute cure; and that is a complete and
overwhelming faith and simple trust in the love and power of
God, in His will and ability to make of every happening in life a
means of ultimate welfare and happiness."[1] When fear threatens
me, God invites me to entrust myself to his loving, powerful
presence. There is nothing that will cause me lasting harm when
I am within his caring protection. This is something I can trust
and take to heart.

Where there is trust in the loving and powerful Presence, the
roots of fear wither. Growing awareness of and reliance on the
reliable care of God leave no room for fear that hinders, let alone
paralyzes. God *is* working everything that has happened together
for my good and for the furtherance of his purposes. He really *is*.
This is something I can count on.

It's said that there is a well-known trio of reactions that fear
provokes in people: fight, flight, or freeze. Freeze and flight have
been my more common reactions. Perhaps yours is to fight.
What might be God's formational invitation in each of these reactions? God might invite the "fighters" to surrender and entrust
themselves to God. Maybe he really does fight *for* us and doesn't
leave us to fight alone. God might invite the "flighters" to return
to him. Rather than hiding, God invites them to abide. And God

might invite the "freezers" to lean into the fear with him. Rather than being immobilized by fears, God invites them to go with him into the fearful place.

GOD WORKS IN YOU

As a young Christian I was often pointed to Paul's words in Philippians 2:12-13 as an encouragement to keep growing and transforming: "Therefore, my dear friends, as you have always obeyed—not only in my presence, but now much more in my absence—continue to work out your salvation with fear and trembling, for it is God who works in you to will and to act in order to fulfill his good purpose." The emphasis was usually on the phrase "work out your salvation." Since I often worked out at the gym or on neighborhood runs, the words "work out" struck a chord. What wasn't highlighted for me then was that whatever we are working *out* in our lives begins as something God is working *in* our lives. An obedient will is the outworking of a God at work within us to have the capacity to will what is good. God has a very good purpose. He is always inviting us into this purpose. His Spirit is doing good in us so that we might do good in our way of life, of relating to others, of work.

The obedience Paul is hoping for here relates to the conflict occurring among his brothers and sisters at Philippi. He's just offered Jesus as a model of such obedience. Jesus didn't demand his rights as God. Rather, he humbled himself and became a servant. This was in keeping with the Father's intent for him. We continue to work out our salvation in the context of the community of God's people too.

And what about this "fear and trembling" language? When I first heard this taught and preached, it sounded something like,

"You had *better* work out your salvation because you have good reason to be fearful and tremble if you fail." It was a reminder of the scary image of God I experienced when I was young. I'm wondering if it isn't something a little more like what my counselor encouraged me to do when I felt fearful and anxious: *take it with you.* Might I work out the realities of my salvation—of this kingdom life I have in Christ—by leaning into that which frightens me and causes me to tremble?

For example, when my work has me doing radio interviews, leadership training, conference speaking, or preaching in churches, I often still feel anticipatory anxiety just beforehand. I could decide that I don't like feeling such anxiety and stop doing this kind of work. I'm free to do that. But I might decide that anxiety isn't my best navigator or counselor in this context and that I don't want it making major life decisions for me. I can take it with me and do what I feel anxious about anyway. That has proven to be a very transforming approach.

I cannot remember a time when my anticipatory anxiety was right about the outcome of a particular speaking engagement. Usually, even within the first few minutes I settle in, feel a flow of God's grace, wisdom, and words, and enjoy a peaceful, joyful, holy energy in the work. If I let anxiety make decisions for me, I'd just avoid those things and never do what I feel deeply called to do. So, perhaps as I lean into places where I feel God calling me to grow and change, I will know that I'm in such a place because I feel at least a little fear and trembling. I don't avoid such places to avoid feeling this way. I lean into them and, in a sense, prove those feelings to be misguided in their dire prediction of future harm or shame.

WHOM SHALL I FEAR?

My self-doubt, anxiety, fear, and insecurity continue to get in my way. When this happens, instead of working out my salvation *with* fear and trembling, I avoid the work by circumventing the fear and trembling. It's not fruitful. I don't feel good about such a choice. It isn't a movement that I'm grateful for or proud of.

Psalm 27 often helps me to reframe a fearful moment. The first lines have become something of a mantra for me as I deal daily with my fears.

> The LORD is my light and my salvation—
> whom shall I fear?
> The LORD is the stronghold of my life—
> of whom shall I be afraid? (Psalm 27:1)

In the place where David feels fearful, he remembers God with him. He remembers just who this God is. When David feels surrounded by darkness, he remembers God is his light. When he feels surrounded by threats, he remembers God is present to save him. When he feels overwhelmed by danger, he remembers that God is a safe place for him to be.

This is the challenge and the opportunity when I feel afraid. I've sometimes had the habit of letting my fear be the biggest thing on my horizon. I can let it spread until it is all I see and feel. And when that happens, I find myself paralyzed or seeking to escape and hide. David doesn't do this. In the face of his fears. David reminds himself of who God is with him.

Does this sound simplistic? I don't think David recalls ideas about God. David remembers, even realizes, the presence of God near. Sometimes this happens for me in a moment of silence. As I'm quiet, the fear looms. It threatens. It seeks to intimidate. But I can turn my attention in the stillness to the very real presence of God in that very place. I am not alone with my fears. I have a powerful and loving Companion in fearful places. When I remember God with me, I somehow slow down inside. My fears begin to fade. My anxieties grow quiet. The hurry of my soul diminishes.

Take another look at David's prayer. Remember that first line? "The LORD is my light and my salvation—whom shall I fear?" David's prayer begins with God. That may not sound like much of an insight, since we assume prayer is *always* language focused on God. But too often, I've begun my prayers with a focus on what I feel threatening me or accusing me or hassling me. But I could begin my prayers with a focus on God as my light, my salvation, and my stronghold. When my prayers start with my fears, sometimes I don't find my way out of them. A vision of God with us cuts to the core of fear that rises up in us. Prayer can become a way into God-focused rather than problem- or fear-focused living.

Many of my fears relate to the unknown. I'm afraid of something out there beyond my vision or maybe behind me somewhere in the dark. When I let my fear come first, I become frantic. But the Lord is my light in any dark place. He is my salvation and will save me in whatever way I need saving, even if I don't know how I need to be saved. He is a safe place for my life.

LIGHTEN YOUR LOAD

Many years ago, I (Gem) was driving to a gathering at a friend's home. It was a ladies' Christmas party/game night and time for the gals to get together and whoop it up. I should have been excited, but all I felt was anxiety. I was in a mood. My life felt heavy. This was back in the days when my kids were young, and life was full and moving fast. There really wasn't anything wrong, I just couldn't see out beyond my four walls. Unfortunately, I was leading the gathering that night. How could I lead from a place of anxiety and a feeling of overload? I was supposed to be a part of an evening that invited joy and fun. If my face looked anything like my feelings, I was in big trouble.

As any young mother driving a minivan knows, the best place to pray can be behind the wheel. So, I cried out to God and told him what he already knew. I was anxious and I wanted to get out from under the weight of it. You know, peace that passes understanding and all that. As I was praying, an image popped into my head. I could see myself wearing a heavy and quite full backpack. Sticking out of the top was my family, like a group of Barbie dolls (or, in my case, Ken dolls).

The meaning was swift and impactful. I was carrying everyone around with me, which is a common trait in women, especially mothers. It feels hardwired into us. But seeing the image of the backpack led me to realize that I had a choice. What would I do with the backpack and its contents? I imagined myself taking the backpack off. But I couldn't simply take it off, set it down on the ground, and walk away. Where's the love in that?

So instead, I took out each member of my Ken-doll family, and, one by one, I handed them to Jesus. I didn't just drop and walk. I acknowledged that Jesus is the One who actually carries them. I didn't have to. As I handed over each family member, my load lightened. What I saw in my mind was actually affecting my emotions and my soul.

By the time I got to the party, I was a different person. I was able to enter the doorway with just me in tow, and not the weight of the world. The peace that surpasses understanding was present.

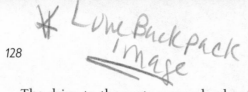

The drive to the party was only about fifteen minutes. You don't always need a lot of time to assess your situation, cry out, and gain some new perspective. Sometimes it can happen in a few minutes, and even while driving.

EXERCISE

If you were to picture a backpack on your shoulders right now, what or who would be in it? Maybe you have a family member who is suffering right now. Perhaps a friend of yours just received devastating news. There may be a work deadline that is keeping you up at night. Not to mention your own insecurities and fears. Take a few minutes and imagine what it would be like if you took those situations and people out of the backpack and handed them to Jesus. What would he do? How would he respond? How might you feel?

FEARS ALONG THE WAY

When we're little the list of things we fear may be quaint: the dark, the boogeyman, spiders, the mean dog next door. However, depending on your family or situation, you may have had next-level fears: the anger of an alcoholic dad, gun shots from the drug house down the street, bullies with hidden knives at school. Nowadays, we have the real fear of public shootings and bombings, even in parts of the country and world that have seemed relatively safe. Add to that the never-ending news threads on our social media feeds, and you have a recipe for constant underlying fear, anxiety, and even dread.

Many of the social issues of our day are the fruit of fear—fear that we won't be taken care of, fear that we won't be seen or loved, fear that we won't have enough. And these dynamics typically lead us directly to fearful or controlling behavior. Looking for and acknowledging our fears feels risky. But if we can come face to face with what we fear, we can see it in the light of God's presence and find healing, freedom, and strength.

In Psalm 81 we read, "I removed the burden from your shoulders; . . . You cried out to Me, I heard your distress, and I delivered you; . . . I am the Eternal, your True God" (Psalm 81:6, 7, 10 *The Voice*). No matter your level of fear or anxiety, the reality is that you are never more than a whispered prayer away from remembering that you are the beloved child of a generous and loving God. Jesus said, "Apart from me you can do nothing." This is not just a statement in the negative. It is an invitation to presence, an invitation to with-ness. Let the love of the Trinity—Father, Son, and Spirit—envelope you so that your fears pale in comparison to the union of relationship.

BE TRANSFORMED

1. How have you dug your own fearful "hippie holes" with an earnest desire to protect yourself? Let God meet you as the Protector in this fearful place.

2. In what ways have you felt shaken? How did you, or how might you, make your way to "My soul finds rest in God alone"?

3. How might you connect with God in your tendency to either fight, flight, or freeze?

4. What or who is in your own metaphorical backpack? What would it look like to hand each person or situation over to Jesus now?

8

CONTROL

WHAT ARE YOU CLINGING TO?

Mystery—*It's okay to not know everything. Some of us breathe a sigh of relief when we see that and others of us break out in hives. Not having the answers can feel quite frustrating. However, the further along you are in your spiritual development, the more comfortable you get with not knowing. We don't even know what we don't know. And that's okay. Rather than maintaining self-contained perspectives, we need God to be bigger than our brain can contain. Mystery allows for that.*

Letting go—*This is one of the greatest keys to peace. Learn to let go. Open your hand and let it fall to the ground. Relax your shoulders, take a breath, and let go. Most of us carry everything around with us at all times. This can be quite overwhelming. Rather than clinging mercilessly to things you cannot change or over which you have no control, simply let go. Literally and figuratively a huge weight will drop as you release and let go.*

A BRAND-NEW CANON 7D, with mysterious buttons and switches everywhere. The black casing was unspoiled and a perfect fit in the inexperienced photographer's hands. As I held that camera, I (Gem) knew that my lifelong dream of learning photography was about to begin. I couldn't wait to dig in. I didn't realize then that my camera would become my lifeline to expression in a season in which I would feel completely out of control.

About the same time that I picked up the camera, I fell into what some have called the "dark night." I was still living my life, working, and caring for my family, but spiritually, everything I thought I knew vanished. The loss of control was overwhelming. I couldn't function the way I normally did. I was left with more questions than answers. I sincerely felt as though I didn't have any helpful counsel for others. Most of my beliefs felt like clichés, and everything went quiet. I could not envision the vocational life I thought I was moving into. I had recently received my first certificate of spiritual direction but decided to put a pause on clients because I felt lost, empty, and as though I had nothing to offer.

It was during this time of no words that I began learning to see. My world shrunk down to what I could see through my camera's viewfinder, and a new door to presence opened. I took my camera everywhere, as it seemed as if all of life was shouting to be seen. I had no words, but my surroundings had plenty to say.

While visiting ancient Gamla in Israel I captured an image of a thistle. I'm fairly certain this plant was a weed. But as I strolled past it on the path, it drew me in with its stark beauty. I swooned over the way the light rimmed the prickly sphere and the various shades of green filled my frame. I loved that I had learned about depth of field, making the background fade away and bringing the thistle into focus. Every time I captured an image like this, my heart would enlarge and my vision would increase. I saw it. I took it in. Its beauty registered in my mind and heart. Even though the rest of me was in a dark night, this part of me, the part that was learning to become present in the moment, came alive.

This is how I was living. Everywhere I went, I watched for the color and temperature of the light. Simple objects would leap out at me and beg to be photographed. Beauty was everywhere, even if beauty was nowhere to be found. In my times of solitude with God, I would often take my camera. In almost every instance, I would recall this phrase from one of my mentors, Chuck Miller: "You are never more creative than when you are with the Creator." I felt as though I was participating in the act of creation. I didn't actually create anything I was seeing, but I was seeing it and capturing it in my own particular way. The line between Creator, creation, and capturer was gone.

That is when I realized I was praying. Chuck Miller also said, "Prayer is not something you do. Prayer is someone you are with." It all became prayer. It was connection without words. I was seeing God in a new way. I was *experiencing* him. The practice of walking slowly, looking through my lens, learning to really see, led easily to presence. I learned to be right where I was, focusing on one thing at a time, taking it in.

LEARNED PRESENCE

Luke 5:16 says that "Jesus often withdrew to lonely places and prayed." It is likely that, at least in part, Jesus was remembering his connection to the Father and how much he was loved. And then he was able to live and minister out of that reality. That is what a season of no words and learned presence are about. They offer a filling that we cannot orchestrate or plan for. In them we learn to be where we are and receive what is there. And at the center of that is God's presence.

No one plans for a dark night. But in a season like that, something can be planted deep within. God guides us along by bringing us to a time of "I don't know" so that he can re-orient our hearts in a revved-down way. Less sense of control. Perhaps when it goes dark in one area, there is room for an unexpected light to shine in another. Perhaps the sense of being out of control becomes the fertile soil for creativity and a new kind of connection with God.

Most of us do not like being out of control. Along with fear, control seems to be at the center of many of our issues. It takes a lot of energy to remain in control at all times. At some point, depending on our stamina, bearing up under the weight of control takes its toll. We find that we are unable to keep going while carrying the world on our shoulders.

What does it take for you to relinquish control? A dark night is certainly one way to deal with control issues. But what are some other ways we can cooperate with God in learning to let go?

We have some friends who are deeply involved in AA and Al-Anon. We learn so much from them as they daily make their way through sobriety, serenity, and letting go. Over the years we've collected some phrases as they've shared with us their wisdom:

I am powerless.

God can restore me to sanity. My best thinking won't get me out.

As best as I can I use my determined willfulness to stop thinking about this.

It is safe for me to let go.

I can make the best decision for me.

These phrases have helped as we learn to let go of control and maintain peace of mind.

CONTROLLING OTHERS

Much of the stress in our lives is caused by expectations, as well as trying to control situations so they turn out the way we think they should. This happens consciously and unconsciously throughout any given day.

For example, a few years ago I (Gem) took two friends to lunch in order to set some things straight.[1] I thought they weren't communicating well with each other, and I wanted to help them see that. I wanted to "make the situation better." If you are good at recognizing foreshadowing, you can see where this is headed. You might have even warned me back then to simply mind my own business. Good counsel. Evidently, I like to learn things the hard way.

I had told both of them before the lunch that I thought they needed to talk and mend their friendship. It is amazing to me now that they both agreed to this. We chitchatted through most of lunch. Near the end, I brought up the subject of their relationship. After a few minutes of halted conversation, one of them sat silently and the other began to get angry at me. The one who was angry finally said, "That's it" and walked out of the restaurant. The other two of us got up and followed. It was over.

This is a very embarrassing story for me. I am embarrassed now because I can see the futility of this situation. I had no right to "take control" and try to fix something that was actually none of my business. It was like a slap in the face. I was awake, and I would never be the same. I wasn't even mad at my two friends. They were right to be upset with me.

On the way to the car I experienced viscerally the meaning of free will. People get to choose how they behave and what they do in their relationships. Everyone gets to decide for themselves how they will act. It was not my job to "make things right." I didn't actually know the whole story. And even if I did, my opinion should have stayed my own unless I was asked for it.

Now, if I find myself having an opinion how a person should behave, I say to myself, "They get to choose how they react, respond, or behave. I don't get to choose that for them." In these phrases I find freedom and a sense of peace for myself. I do not need to control people. I can let go. As the Al-Anon saying goes, "I work on keeping my own side of the street clean."

Yes, we all have situations in our lives that aren't going the way we want. But much of the anxiety we carry is actually brought on by our own fears and a desire for control. We want to put our fears to rest, so we try to control people and situations.

Most of us already know that control is an illusion. We do not get to control other people. Every person gets to choose how they act, what they say, and how they deal with their own lives. I've learned this the hard way, after many years of unconscious holding on. Letting go is one of the greatest gifts you can give yourself. A new realm of peace can open up for you. Letting go is a process, and the loving arms of God are a good place to start. In him we live, move, and have our being.

Where are you tempted to control another person or situation? Where are you resisting God's life-giving invitation to surrender, let go, and trust? Control is the enemy of peace, joy, and love. Whether we are single or married, have children or not, it seems that there is always someone or something in our lives that we feel the need to control. The invitation is to awaken to the reality that control is an illusion. There is only one Sovereign . . . and it isn't me. When we try to control other people, they have a way of dashing our expectations to the ground. This is where loving detachment comes in. We discover that our control issues are doing more real harm than the good we envisioned. It can be hard to admit that we are grasping onto someone so fiercely. But if we will let ourselves see it, and work through it, we can find our way into a place of greater joy and peace.

SELF-ABANDONMENT TO DIVINE PROVIDENCE

Many years ago, when I (Alan) was discovering a more prayerful way to live and to do my work, I stumbled across an unexpected book in a store I didn't usually visit. It was a rather thick volume with a fairly ominous sounding title, *Self-Abandonment to Divine Providence*. (More contemporary versions of this work have been published under the title *The Sacrament of the Present Moment*.) The author was a spiritual director from the early eighteenth century by the name of Jean-Pierre de Caussade. The book consisted of a hundred-page essay followed by about 150 letters of spiritual direction based on it.

Like any three-hundred-year-old book, not everything I read seemed helpful or easily practiced in light of present-day sensibilities or assumptions. There was wisdom in it that sometimes felt a bit hard to swallow. The language of "self-abandonment" does not sound like a fruitful or inviting way to live one's life when self-fulfillment seems the order of the day.

For years, one of the ways I've enjoyed digesting and applying what I'm learning in a good book is to write out meaningful quotations from it and then reflect prayerfully on them in my journal. I'll usually gather a page or two of quotations I've found helpful. When I read *Self-Abandonment to Divine Providence*, I wrote out seventeen pages of quotations. Just those excerpts would be two or three chapters in the average book. I think my strong response to what Jean-Pierre was saying was rooted in my intuitive sense that I had a problem with control, and that he was addressing it directly and wisely.

Abandoning ourselves sounds like a loss, but I've experienced it as freedom. I've found it a pretty miserable thing to be a slave to my own whims, impulses, urges, or itches. Demanding this sort of autonomy or control has not proven to be the freedom I thought it would be. Trying to control something I don't have the power to control is a great burden, one I carry far too often. Freedom has actually come as I've given up control and lovingly offered myself to the good will of Another.

I found myself recently saying to a young man with whom I meet regularly, "The ideal situation in which to grow spiritually is your life now, exactly as you find it." Clinging to some ideal situation that is other than where I find myself doesn't bear good fruit. This is the spirit of what I learned from Jean-Pierre. The grace of God is not more available in another place or in someone else's life. God is with you here and now in your particular, unique life.

> The ideal situation in which to grow spiritually is your life now, exactly as you find it.

Now, sometimes I believe that sentence for myself and sometimes I struggle to embrace it. Part of me imagines I'd find it far easier to grow in my life with God in a different set of circumstances, or with a different set of temperamental bents. I imagine that I need a change in venue, and I try to *make* that happen. But Jesus is such a masterful mentor and guide that he is able to provide the right transforming counsel in exactly the situation, outward and inward, in which I find myself. Jean-Pierre encourages us that "God reveals himself to the humble in the humblest things, while the great who never penetrate beneath the surface do not discover him even in great events."[2] Transformation is not a journey reserved for an imagined spiritual elite. No matter how small or humble we may feel, Jesus is inviting us on the remarkable journey with him into transformation in his image.

On the theme of transformation, Jean-Pierre tells us, "God's designs, God's good pleasure, the will of God, the action of God and his grace are all one and the same thing in this life. They are God working in the soul to make it like himself. Perfection is nothing else than the faithful co-operation of the soul with the work of God, and it begins, grows and is consummated in our souls secretly and without our being aware of it."[3] Transformation is the fruit of God's pleasure, God's intentions, God's purposes, and God's work, which are not different things but facets of a single rich divine reality.

How do we cooperate with God's good, beautiful, and inviting purposes? Jean-Pierre tells us that "divine action, being limitless in its plenitude, can take possession of a soul only to the extent to which that soul is emptied of all trust in its own action, for such self-confidence is a spurious fullness that excludes divine action."[4] We want to get control of our transformation and cling to personal strategies of how to make it happen. It's as though we're trying to transform ourselves *for* God rather than being transformed *by* God. Transformation happens within us and bears fruit outwardly. It is a work of God with which we are invited to cooperate.

God's grace is limitless, and yet we can unintentionally oppose it in the misguided pride of our clinging, controlling self-confidence (or at least self-reliance). As Jean-Pierre suggests, when we are full of our own designs, our own pleasures, our own will, and our own activities, we find ourselves unexpectedly resistant to the working of God's generous and empowering grace. Sometimes, my implicit prayer when it comes to change has ended up as something like, "Lord, change me . . . as long as I can be in control of how it happens." Trusting abandonment of ourselves to God's good work is a path to being deeply transformed. Frantic activity to change ourselves doesn't grow very deep roots.

Jesus taught his followers to pray, "Your kingdom come, your will be done, on earth as it is in heaven" (Matthew 6:10). But I sometimes live as though my primary aim is "my kingdom come, my will be done." I can even do this under the guise of doing it all "for God." I end up spending a lot of time determining how I will be in charge of the outcomes of my life. I try to control circumstances. I even try to control others. This requires an immense amount of energy, and it isn't energy well spent. Transformation is not building my own kingdom, but welcoming and entering into a much more magnificent, beautiful, glorious kingdom ruled by Another.

I've noticed this tendency to "build my own kingdom" in certain video games I've been drawn to. I like strategy games. Nothing wrong with that. But what I'm drawn to is a feeling of being in control, leadership even, of someone or something. In many of the games I play, I'm deciding how to arrange an army or build a city or defend against an imagined enemy. I think it's an expression of my misguided desire for control. And when I don't feel like I can control my actual life in ways I expect, I resort to gaining a degree of control or mastery in an imaginary world. But I might actually find the kind of authority and power I'm hungry for in the service of God's leadership and sovereign power. There is something rich and real in the authority I experience in humble friendship with God that far surpasses any imagined or pretend authority.

THE BROKEN CONTAINER

The prophet Jeremiah says on God's behalf to a very wayward Israel: "My people have committed two sins: They have forsaken me, the spring of living water, and have dug their own cisterns, broken cisterns that cannot hold water" (Jeremiah 2:13). These two sins are like two sides of the same coin. They wanted control of their own lives. They said no to the divine invitation to abundant life and refreshment and instead tried to create and hold a life of their own. Jeremiah uses this image to tell them that their effort to take control of their own lives amounted to trying to store water in a broken container. Even more tragic, they were doing it in full view of a spring of living water. God was inviting them to a relationship of trust (springs), but Israel was trying to control their own lives (cistern). Trust is a doorway through which God's empowering and God's blessing flow into us and through us to bless others. Since God is the One who transforms our lives, trust is a way of welcoming God's work in us.

> Trust is a doorway through which God's empowering and God's blessing flow into us and through us to bless others.

Eugene Peterson helps us understand the relationship between trust and control: "Faith has to do with marrying Invisible and Visible. When we engage in an act of faith we give up control, we give up sensory (sight, hearing, etc.) confirmation of reality; we give up insisting on head-knowledge as our primary means of orientation in life."[5] Our attempts to take control are a way to live as though only what we can see matters. But God is invisible to us. We may witness the impact of his presence and his work in the world around us, but sometimes we struggle to see him.

When it comes to control, God doesn't wish to force our hand. David speaks on God's behalf in Psalm 32:

> I will instruct you and teach you in the way you should go;
>   I will counsel you with my loving eye on you.
> Do not be like the horse or the mule,
>   which have no understanding
> but must be controlled by bit and bridle
>   or they will not come to you. (Psalm 32:8-9)

God doesn't want to control us like a rider might control a horse with bit and bridle. God invites us to offer ourselves freely to him with love and trust.

I imagine God speaking this to me personally: "Alan, I see your waywardness and your wrongdoing. If you would let me, I would teach you how to really live. I would counsel you from a posture and perspective of love. I don't want to control you like a stubborn mule. I want to lead you like a son. Let me lead you, Alan." Trust like this opens the way for us to be deeply changed. We learn to trust the Father in the very way Jesus trusted (and trusts) the Father.

We see a beautiful example of this trust in Mary's response to the angel Gabriel when he announces to her that she will conceive a child apart from a husband and by the power of the Holy

Spirit: "Behold, I am the servant of the Lord; let it be to me according to your word" (Luke 1:38 ESV). This is the opposite of the impulse to control. Surely Mary might have preferred to have some control over how she would bear her first child, which makes her humble response to God's messenger all the more remarkable and beautiful. God had spoken puzzling words to her. But she had come to know God as good, beautiful, and true. She trusted God, and so she abandoned controlling the path she would have chosen and entrusted herself to a path God was offering her.

When God gave Gem and me a vision in our twenties of sharing our lives with leaders as a major element of our ministry work in the future, we thought we knew what that meant. We were ready to take control of that vision and "make it happen." We had definite ideas and even expectations about how that would happen. God had given us a vision of "what," but we were taking it on ourselves to control the "how." But God wasn't giving me an assignment to do for him. He was inviting me to a life lived in communion with him. He was inviting me to be changed into the kind of person who could live into and live out of this vocational vision. Learning how to abandon myself to his care, guidance, and empowering presence was going to be a major chapter of my life.

Along the way, I learned that the path of transformation lies in the direction of increasing trust in the loving power of God to do exactly what he promises to do. This is not a movement in the direction of more control for me, but less. It is, in a sense, a return to the loving dependence in which we were created in Eden. One way of understanding our disobedience in the garden is humans choosing our own "I will" in the face of God's "I will."

to my own will hasn't been a fruitful thing in my life.
d transformation have come in learning to cling to
God ... and to hold everyone and everything else more loosely.
Transformation is not a white-knuckle activity as much as an openhanded one.

Ironically, letting go of control has moved me in the direction of greater security and peace. I feared I'd have less of these if I felt less in control. Yet the secret to peace is found in abandonment to the loving care of God. I assumed that more control would lead to more peace, but it has instead led to more anxiety and fear. I somehow intuitively know that trying to wrap my arms around everything to gain the illusion of control leaves me alone trying to manage my life. While self-control is a fruit of the Spirit, selfish-control is not. "I can do it myself" is a lonely way to live. God invites us instead to live in the rich communion of "We can do this together." I love how Dallas Willard explained the dynamics of this:

> If grace and wisdom prevail in the life of the one who only surrenders to God's will, he or she will move on to abandonment. Then the individual is fully surrendered. There is no longer any part of himself or herself that holds back from God's will. . . . We therefore no longer fret over "the bad things that happen to good people," though we may undergo much hardship and suffering. While [God] does not cause these things to happen, we now accept them as within his plan for good to those who love him and are living in his purposes (Romans 8:28). Irredeemable harm does not befall those who willingly live in the hand of God.[6]

Returning to the language of clinging reminds me of the way a branch remains closely connected to a vine. Jesus used this image when he spoke of our relationship with him, saying, "I am the vine; you are the branches. If you remain in me and I in you, you will bear much fruit; apart from me you can do nothing" (John 15:5). I've learned that my attempt to take control of things on my own is a way of clinging to the wrong vine. Jesus says that he is the true vine, which implies that there are false vines. I cling to a false vine when I try to draw my life, my purpose, my energy from someone or something other than Jesus. I do this in so many ways. I try to control things around me and my own life by making my own plans, taking my own way, controlling my own outcomes.

Another word in the vocabulary of releasing control and learning to trust is *obedience*. Like *self-abandonment, submission,* or *surrender, obedience* is a word many of us have a deep suspicion and resistance to. But as I enter into these responses to God, I find myself humbly surprised. It turns out to be a joy to follow the guidance, direction, and instructions of God as I realize just how good, caring, and wise God is. I'm happy to trust in and follow the direction of a fitness coach who is fit, skilled, compassionate, and confident. Such "obedience" bears good fruit. How much more does obeying the counsel of our Father in heaven bear good fruit?

So God invites me to obedience to his loving wisdom. He invites me to leave childish ways behind and grow in maturity by following his direction, his counsel, his training. This is another facet of my transforming journey. In Christ, God invites us to walk with him, stay with him, be changed in loving relationship with him.

> Obedience and confidence go together.

Obedience and confidence go together. When I go my own way, I go alone. When I walk with God, I go forward in good company.

LIKE A LITTLE CHILD

"The opposite of love is control. Show me someone who has given up power and control, and I'll show you someone close to sanctity." This insight came from my (Gem) first spiritual director, Abbot David. He would then add, "Truly I tell you, unless you change and become like little children, you will never enter the kingdom of heaven" (Matthew 18:3). In this regard, we connect to God not merely with our heads but with our hearts and our inner child.

Abbot David was a "what you see is what you get" (WYSIWYG) kind of person. A while back I was sitting with my next spiritual director, and we were reminiscing about Abbot David, who passed away a few years ago. We were both moved to tears remembering what it was like to be in his presence. He was, and still is, my poster child for WYSIWYG living.

Highly intelligent, Abbot David was engaging and guileless, with such an ease about him. One of my favorite activities was saying something funny enough to get him to laugh. It made my day. His entire face lit up, his eyes crinkled, and his laugh came from deep within. I sensed a purity of presence that led to such joy being with him. There was no ego and no need to control. He was childlike in the best sense of the word. He had nothing to prove and nothing to lose, and so to be with him was captivating and peaceful.

I've been struck by a section on childlikeness in Dallas Willard's *The Divine Conspiracy*:

> Interestingly, "growing up" is largely a matter of learning to hide our spirit behind our face, eyes, and language so that we can evade and manage others to achieve what we want and avoid what we fear. By contrast, the child's face is a constant epiphany because it doesn't yet know how to do this. It cannot manage its face. This is also true of adults in moments of great feeling—which is one reason why feeling is both greatly treasured and greatly feared.
>
> Those who have attained considerable spiritual stature are frequently noted for their "childlikeness." What this really means is that they do not use their face and body to hide their spiritual reality. In their body they are genuinely present to those around them. This is a great spiritual attainment or gift.[7]

What if, as Abbot David and Dallas Willard suggest, the key to letting go of control is being more childlike? There is a kind of presence that we experience when we are with people of "spiritual stature." We experience them this way because they do not hide or unnecessarily control their true selves.

The person who hides can sometimes tend to control and manage others and also avoid what they fear. And here they are again: *control* and *fear*. Control and fear are so basic to our disease, unhealth, and lack of peace. Over time, however, I am learning to let myself see things as they truly are, learning to loosen my grip on managing other people's behavior, and learning to overcome my fears.

THE HUMBLE WAY OF TRANSFORMATION

When attempting to engage healing in the arena of control there are three simple words that have helped me make my way: *small, simple,* and *gracious*.[8] Control is such a sneaky and insidious beast that coming at it with full force usually backfires. So these kinds of moves are best.

Small. If you notice yourself seeking to grab control in a certain situation, pause for a moment and see if you can find a way forward that is as small as possible. Not heroic. Not earth-shaking. Small. When you are making a change, it's the habit that is critically important, and small makes developing a habit more likely to stick.

Simple. Along with small, it's best if our response is also simple. Not complicated or dramatic. So simple that you could describe it to a third grader and they would understand. Simple keeps it real, and real means your change has a chance to grow and flourish.

Gracious. Graciousness seems a lost art in our current culture. Communication is loud and in-your-face, contempt is rampant, and opinions pose as truth. Graciousness takes a breath and takes the sting out of our movements. Judgment is laid aside, and we can remain with our chosen path of healing in the area of control.

In Romans 12 there are a couple of verses that continue to help with all of this: "So since we find ourselves fashioned into all these excellently formed and marvelously functioning parts in Christ's body, *let's just go ahead and be what we were made to be*, without enviously or pridefully comparing ourselves with each other, or trying to be something we aren't. . . . *Love from the center of who you are*" (Romans 12:6, 9 *The Message*, emphasis added).

I came upon these passages one day as I was preparing to lead a retreat. I felt nervous, and I was trying to hold all of my content in my memory and keep it there so that I felt in control of the day. When I cannot achieve this in a way that makes me feel safe, I get overly anxious. This is, of course, not the way to become a safe, hospitable host for women seeking God on a retreat day.

When I saw the first phrase, "Let's just go ahead and be who we were made to be," I said to myself, *I can do that. I can be me.* And I relaxed a bit. And as I read "Love from the center of who you are," I knew I could do that too. I let go of the need to memorize, manage, and control the content, and I relaxed into these two doable invitations from God. *Be who I am* and *love from the center of who I am.* I can do both of those things. And isn't this at least, in part, what it means to be childlike? Toddlers do this in spades. They are who they are, and they love without holding back. I now recall these verses often before I engage in public speaking, and I let them quell any control or fear issues that may arise.

Being who I am and loving from the center of who I am are both small, simple, and gracious. I understand them, and I can easily connect with how to realistically live them. They take the sting out of my control issues, so I can simply be myself and be awake to what is happening right in front of me, just like a child. People like Abbot David Geraets and Dallas Willard embodied this at another level. I pray that I can attain even half the measure of presence they attained while on this earth. I pray this for you as well. As we open ourselves up more and more to God's love and transformative power, let's allow God to guide us in the way of childlikeness that leads to letting go of control.

BE TRANSFORMED

Health

1. What makes you feel the most out of control? How might you meet God there?

2. What would it look like if you decided that the people in your life get to choose how they react, respond, or behave?

3. "The ideal situation in which to grow spiritually is your life now, exactly as you find it." What are your thoughts about this statement? How does this speak to any desire to control that you might be feeling?

4. "Let it be to me according to your word." How might you foster a sense of humility like Mary, the mother of Jesus? How might that level of trust emerge from within you?

 # awareness

9

JOY

WHAT DOES YOUR SOUL LOVE?

Flow—Instead of thinking of yourself as one who cranks out goods and services, let yourself be a vessel for filling and for overflow. God's love, flowing from within, out toward others. This assumes that you are in a receptive mode with God and then in an overflowing mode toward others. In the center is you being blessed by God and blessed by serving. It's about love and relationship rather than pushing.

WHEN I (GEM) WANTED TO EXPERIENCE a sense of freedom and joy as a young girl, I would head straight for the pasture of our six-acre homestead. I would make my way out to our barbed-wire fence and call for Lady, my Palomino horse. She had been a parade horse until she retired and came to live on our small farm. I owned, but rarely used, the black leather and silver-studded saddle and bridle that she wore as she rode in front of the waving crowds.

During the summer months, when I called Lady, she would trot over to me so I could climb on her bare back. I would grab her blond mane, hunker down, tap her sides gently with my little feet, and we were off, with my long, dark hair waving in the wind. Our entire pasture was fenced, so I was safe to roam freely, walking, trotting, and galloping as I pleased.

There was nothing like the feeling of being astride a galloping horse on a lazy summer day. It created such a sense of freedom and joy. Idyllic really. Sun on my back, wind in my face, and being carried along by a trustworthy friend.

Sometimes Lady and I would trot along the perimeter. We would pass our small barn on the left that was outlined with blackberry bushes. We would then curve around the back corner and pass the home of Mr. and Mrs. Linch, my pseudo-grandparents. Mrs. Linch was a German baker and would always call my mom when she made a fresh batch of some decadent pastry.

After the Linchs' house, Lady and I would make our way along the fence that bordered the street, past our small pond and our apple tree, and then I'd be back to the gate where I started. The pasture was about four acres, and it was all mine as I rode. Sometimes I would ride back and forth, galloping across the pasture. But whichever way I made my way across the pasture, I was always safe within its boundaries. A barbed-wire fence made sure of that. I was safe, and I could go where I wanted within our property.

Another enjoyable summer event was attending the local county fair as a family. We'd make our way through the exhibits of ribbon-adorned handmade quilts, homemade pies, bleating livestock, and sales people hawking the latest gadget. And, of course, there were the rides. I especially loved the huge yellow slide with all of its lanes and hills.

One year, my dad and I decided to go into a fun house just before leaving the fair for the day. We made our way inside, and it was pitch black. It turned out to be a dark maze. We should have turned around right then, but we continued to make our way through, feeling the walls and bumping into most of them. At one point, we hit a wall and a small square lit up with a scary clown face in it. Pair that with an extraordinarily loud buzzer, and you've got a real moment of terror. I screamed and flailed and couldn't wait to get out of there. Why in the world did they call it a fun house? That was no fun at all.

JOY BEYOND CIRCUMSTANCE

In my early years as a Christian, I was under the impression that the Christian life was like that fun-house maze. There was one, predetermined way through all of the high walls, and if you didn't engage it properly you would find yourself at a dead end, with no hope of making your way through. Or worse, you'd find yourself scared to death because you went the wrong way.

As I've grown older, I've come to realize that the Christian life is more like the pasture from my childhood home than that scary fairground maze. Sure, there is a fence that surrounds the pasture, but there is plenty of space in which to explore and enjoy. I can go anywhere at any time and be completely safe. There is a feeling of freedom and joy within my pleasant boundaries.

In John 10 Jesus describes himself as the Gate *and* the Good Shepherd. He lets us in and out of the fold, calls us by name, and goes with us. The pasture of freedom and joy is this shepherd-guarded space inside our pleasant boundaries. We have the freedom to run, play, and express ourselves within that large space. We don't have to worry so much about the heavy burden and fears of the maze of the Christian life. Walking with God and growing in kingdom ways shapes our desires, and we begin to love God's ways more naturally, so that even the pleasant boundaries feel like freedom.

The kingdom of God is a place of great joy. It's the most joyful realm that exists. The apostle Paul says a lot about joy, yet of all the apostles, his situation often seemed the least pleasant and the most difficult. We see this juxtaposition in his letter to the church at Philippi. It's full of references to his joy even though he's writing it from prison (Philippians 1:13-14). He's deeply glad that the message of the gospel continues to make progress even in his captivity, and even in the face of some who preached it almost spitefully to make him jealous (Philippians 1:15-17).

> Walking with God and growing in kingdom ways shapes our desires, and we begin to love God's ways more naturally, so that even the pleasant boundaries feel like freedom.

The old Paul, called Saul, would have responded much differently than the transformed Paul does. Saul would have probably been vengeful. Paul is joyful. His circumstances do little to inspire joy, yet he is joyful.

In three different places in his letter, Paul uses a simple little phrase: "Rejoice in the Lord" (Philippians 3:1; 4:4 twice). Paul isn't excited about his situation as much as he is joyful in God with him in that situation. It is a joy *in* more than a joy *about*. This inner, relational joy energizes transformation and is the fruit of a communion with God like Paul experiences.

The kind of joy Paul talks about is not the result of a pleasant situation that resonates easily with my personal preferences. Pleasurable moments make me happy. Paul's joy is a deep sense of the energizing and buoyant nature of his kingdom home that bubbles up from the depths of his soul. His joy is relational rather than circumstantial.

Of the eight questions we discuss in this book, "What does your soul love?" is one of the more challenging ones for me (Alan). I too often substitute external stimulation for internal life and energy. I sometimes seek excitement over joy. But the joy of God's kingdom rises up from within us. Rather than a response to something outside of us, joy is a lightness and an energy that bubbles up from the place of being at home in the presence of a God who smiles easily.

The psalms speak of this same sort of joy. David says to the Lord, "[People] feast on the abundance of your house; you give them drink from your river of delights. For with you is the fountain of life; in your light we see light" (Psalm 36:8-9). There is a river of delights in the presence of God. There is an abundant feast when we trust and experience God with us. Joy and delight bubble up from within us as God is more and more at home in us and we in God.

I'm tempted to think that delight and joy are something I have to seek somewhere out there. But the joyful presence of God is not somewhere else. God is here, and so joy is right here, too. One of the patterns that joy transforms in me is my old habit of assuming scarcity. If I'd let him, Jesus would mentor me into living in the truth of the abundant kingdom that is my home. I am learning to see my life and work through this lens, rather than through the grey, cracked lens of scarcity. I learn that my hungers and thirsts have a reliable and lavish source of provision. I come to see my life as surrounded by more good things than I can hold. I have *very* good reason to be joyful.

Transformation moves me in the direction of recognizing greater inner abundance. I learn to be oriented to having more good available to me, here and now, than I can hold. I learn to resist the temptation to think that the *more* I am hungry for is out there somewhere. This present abundance is rich with energizing joy.

In another psalm, David begins his prayer with these words: "My heart, O God, is steadfast; I will sing and make music with all my soul" (Psalm 108:1). A steadfast heart is a wonderful place from which to engage our journey of transformation into the image of God. A steadfast heart is the opposite of a distracted heart, a shaky heart, or a timid heart. A steadfast heart is joyful and free. I'm hungry for a heart more steadfast in God than it has sometimes been. I need to be rooted and established in God so that my life and my work each day is an expression of joyful, even melodic, praise.

In yet another David song, he prays in this way: "The whole earth is filled with awe at your wonders; where morning dawns, where evening fades, you call forth songs of joy" (Psalm 65:8). God inspires and invites songs of joy from the earliest moments of morning light to the very last moments of fading twilight. From the beginning to the end of my day, this joy is a response to the wonder of God with us. His wonders, when we slow down to become more fully awake to them, inspire profound awe and delight. For example, as I am writing this morning, I can hear the joyful songs of my neighborhood birds. There is the multi-toned song of the mockingbird, the screeching shout of a bright yellow male oriole, the high-pitched peep of the hummingbirds, and the quieting coo of a mother dove on her nest. They are the sound of joy to me.

The joy that is a path to transformation is a response to the awesome, glorious, and joyful presence of God with us. It is a smile that is rooted in the depths of our being where God is very much at home in us. This is a joy we can bring into our relationships and our work. It isn't a joy that we're seeking somewhere out there at some distance from ourselves. This joy strengthens us in our depths for the journey of transformation.

> The joy that is a path to transformation is a response to the awesome, glorious, and joyful presence of God with us.

DRAWING NEAR TO GOD

In order to experience this joy that leads to transformation, we must draw near to God. The story of Nehemiah offers wisdom for us on what that looks like. Nehemiah's message seems to be mainly about urging God's people to draw near rather than live at such a distance from God as they'd done for so long. The people of God stood as a community as Ezra the priest read aloud from the Book of the Law (see Nehemiah 8). They were listening to the words, the counsel, the instruction, the ways of their God read aloud. And they were painfully, grievously awakened to how short they had fallen from the life to which God had been inviting them.

In our own journeys of transformation, we may draw near to God to listen to what God says to us in the Scriptures, and we, too, might realize how short we come to living fully into the reality they speak of. But God does not want us to become mired in such grief. Listen to the counsel God gave his people through Nehemiah that day: "Nehemiah said, 'Go and enjoy choice food and sweet drinks, and send some to those who have nothing prepared. This day is holy to our Lord. Do not grieve, for the joy of the LORD is your strength'" (Nehemiah 8:10). This day in which they were hearing God's counsel and realizing how little of it they had taken to heart was a very holy day. God was not demanding their regrets. God was inviting them to gratitude, to joy, even to a celebration. God wanted them to experience this as a day of joyful discovery.

Joy really is the place God wants me to make myself at home. Joy doesn't disregard painful realities about personal failures, shortcomings, or line-crossings. Joy is holy energy moving us in the direction of transformation. Lingering grief, especially over all the ways we aren't who we could be, can become draining and corrosive to our souls. I say this as a particularly scrupulous soul. Self-condemnation has too often come too easily for me.

> Joy is holy energy moving us in the direction of transformation.

But condemnation is never the voice of the Father, and it isn't the genuine voice of the new me made in the image of the Son.

God's joy strengthens us. Joy is the source of vital kingdom energy. The kingdom of God is full of joy because God is joyful. The fruit of the Spirit is joy because God is joyful. I have often struggled to envision God as this joyful a person. In my imagination, God has sometimes looked like a human father having a bad day or a distant authority making unreasonable and heartless demands. But God is truly joyful, and that joy energizes us. God wants us to know and trust this. Again, if the fruit of the Spirit, which is a sign of our transformation, includes joy, then this is because God is joyful. Do I embrace this as the nature of the God in whom I live, work, and exist? Such a vision of God will surely transform us.

This brings to mind words of encouragement and comfort that Jesus spoke to his inner circle on the night he would be arrested: "As the Father has loved me, so have I loved you. Now remain in my love. If you keep my commands, you will remain in my love, just as I have kept my Father's commands and remain in his love. I have told you this so that my joy may be in you and that your joy may be complete. My command is this: Love each other as I have loved you" (John 15:9-12). The disciples didn't know quite what was about to happen, but Jesus knew that their grief would be great. He wanted them to be prepared with a great vision of the love of the Father for him, of his love for the Father, and of their great affection for these followers. This vision of profound love would enable them to know and trust in the joy of Jesus. Jesus wanted them (and us) to know the joy he knows and feels. He wanted them to enter fully into *his* joy, to be energized and moved by such joy into everything good he wanted them to enjoy and then to share with others.

When we assume that joy is something out there that we need to go find, joy becomes an elusive chase. But what if all the joy I could hope for is already here because God is already here? What if my joy is a relationship in which to deepen rather than a frantic search for a prize that's playing hard to get? Joy is not some consumer good I'm trying to get enough of. Joy is a reality of the soul of which I have an abundant supply. Holy joy changes us as we do what we do day to day. Joy is an engine for transformation.

Jesus tells us that we will remain in his love if we keep the commands the Father has given him, and us through him. Joy enables us to realize that obedience isn't grudgingly doing what someone else says. Joy is recognizing that our truest heart is already in agreement with the life God is inviting us to.

Obedience becomes a willing, loving choice to agree with God and to join him in his way. I obey God joyfully because I believe God is inviting me into real and deep joy.

Of course, this requires trust. We may not see right away how a particular directive from God will lead us into places of rich and overflowing life. There may be part of us that disagrees with his counsel. Obviously, there is a part of me that still believes that the comfort or joy or satisfaction I long for is out there somewhere. But what I need is not mostly out there but mostly right here with God.

All of this is important because there are times when it's simply impossible to find a reason for joy in our circumstances. The closing lines of Habakkuk's prophecy express how little reason for happiness he has around him: "Though the fig tree does not blossom, and no fruit is on the vines; though the produce of the olive fails, and the fields yield no food; though the flock is cut off from the fold, and there is no herd in the stalls, yet I will rejoice in the LORD; I will exult in the God of my salvation" (Habakkuk 3:17-18 NRSV). Can you feel the heaviness of his repeated, "Though, though, though"? He looks around and sees fig trees, grapevines, olive trees, and fields all failing to be productive in ways he wanted (or even felt he needed). He looks around and there are no sheep in the fold or any herds of cattle in the stalls. Nothing is fruitful. Nothing is productive.

Do you ever feel like that? Do you ever look around and feel that just about everything is going wrong? Do you feel like there just isn't anything worth feeling happy about? Habbakuk can empathize. So can I.

"Though" speaks to circumstances and situations that are unfavorable, unpleasant, unwelcome. Everything following Habakkuk's "though" is something we don't want or welcome. But Habakkuk doesn't stop at "though." He moves through it to "yet." He says, "Yet I will rejoice." "Yet" speaks to a source of joy that comes from beyond our transitory or temporary hardships. They feel like forever, but they really aren't. Habakkuk invites us to choose joy even when the outcome of our work or the nature of our circumstances is beyond disappointing. Joy like this becomes fuel for a changed perspective and a transforming life. My circumstances are never the last word of my life or my joy. Ever. Period.

This was a reality that John the Baptist seemed to understand. When some who had been his followers left to begin following Jesus, this could have been a source of sorrow or a sign of loss. But he responded by saying, "The bride belongs to the bridegroom. The friend who attends the bridegroom waits and listens for him, and is full of joy when he hears the bridegroom's voice. That joy is mine, and it is now complete. He must become greater; I must become less" (John 3:29-30). Isn't John's response beautiful? He's just been told that people are leaving him and going over to Jesus to follow him. He is "losing his influence" to Jesus. It's a funny thing to say, and it's not at all how John saw things. Jesus is the bridegroom. God's people are the bride. And John understands that he is an honored friend present as a witness. The bride belongs to the groom and not to the friend.

Can you imagine a wedding where one of the groomsmen complained that the bride and the groom were getting all the attention? The groomsman, like us, is there to serve, not to draw attention. This is our source of joy. Joy and humility are good friends. Our privileged place in this whole thing is as a joyful witness. This is the kind of joy that transforms us into the gentle, humble image of Jesus.

JOY AND VARIETY

Discipline can be good and necessary when we want to get something accomplished. But in the work of the soul, sometimes it's good to follow the breadcrumbs of desire through the forest of transformation in order to make our way to our heart's home. For a time, we can engage in spiritual practices that connect us with more joy and beauty in our relationship with God. This can rejuvenate us in a season when we experience everything as a pressure—as expectation rather than relationship.

When we participate in a soul-filling practice, it's good to remember the key idea is that we are *with God*. Whatever we do, remembering that we are with God can make it a part of our ongoing transformation. We are trying to move away from the mindset of assignments, to-do lists, and any hint of duty.

Some people are disciplined in every aspect of their life. They are able to plan for what foods are best to eat and then stick to it. They decide to work out three times a week and then they do it. They commit to spending one hour each morning with God and they check it off daily. Others are more spontaneous. As soon as they make a plan for themselves, they are bored with it and want to move on or rebel. They get things done but in a more unstructured way.

Feeling trapped is not good for the soul (remember that dark maze?). God is bigger than any rigid list of what it means to connect with him. He is the Creator of the universe, highly imaginative, and, as Dallas Willard has said, "the most joyful being in the universe." God has the extraordinary capacity to be highly creative as he meets with us and grows us over a lifetime.

When I (Gem) was a young mom with a toddler and nursing baby, I began to experience time with God differently than I had as a young married woman with no children. One day, I was sitting in a rocking chair in my bedroom, nursing one of my sons, enjoying the bonding that happens during that time. The peacefulness of those moments is unlike any other. My sole responsibility in that moment was to focus on my baby. With all three of my sons, one of my favorite soothing techniques was to stroke the soft skin between their eyebrows as their eyes would gently close. What a miraculous connection and God-given gift. In that moment, I remember very distinctly a small voice whispering in my ear, "You know, this counts."

Prior to this, I had been accustomed to following my good Christian girl to-do list fairly well. But all of that went out the window moving from one child to two. I loved being a mom, but I couldn't figure out how to spend time with God the way I had before. "You know, this counts" was God's gentle way of saying, "I see you. I know what season of life you are in right now. This moment, with your son—this is how I feel about you. The care you are giving him is good and right. This counts. I am with you. You are with me."

Every once in a while, over the course of my life, I would hear the whisper again, "You know, this counts." It may have been a worship song that was playing in the background or a word of encouragement from a trusted friend. God was showing me that we were together and relating in far more ways than I was giving "credit" for. I didn't have the vocabulary for it then, but I see that as one of my initial awakenings into *with-ness*. A real live version of Immanuel, God with us.

The "parent of young children" season of life made me tired, scattered, and seemingly not in control of my schedule. But God wanted to show me that being *with* him, in the midst of my very real life, mattered and counted. This dynamic can create real, simple joy in the day-to-dayness of our lives.

SOUL-FILLING OPTIONS

So here's a question: What brings joy to your soul? Another way to ask this is, What does your soul love? Instead of tackling the Christian life as a long list of to-dos and measuring sticks, we can get in touch with what we truly love, that which brings us joy. We then meet God there. We can train our souls to engage in the beauty and life around us. It is in paying attention to the small and seemingly mundane in our lives that we can find inexpressible joy.

Here are a few that bring me joy: Zippers. The color red. The smell of a baby's hair. A jar full of M&Ms. A giraffe's long neck. The fragrance of the ground after a rain. The sound crickets make by a campfire. Ocean waves lapping. A sunrise.

Or how about these: The graceful moves of a dancer. People who have been married for sixty-five years. The purple stripe in the neighbor girl's blond hair. Chocolate melting on your tongue. The silence of falling snow. Cold, crisp watermelon on a hot summer's day.[1]

It's okay to spend a bit of time out in the pasture, galloping on a horse with the wind in your hair. By that I mean it's okay to engage spiritual practices that are life giving, practices that bring you joy, that let you experience the fullness of the land on which you find yourself. The question "What does your soul love?" can breathe new life into a season in which you may feel stodgy or stuck or lifeless.

Those of you who truly desire to make your way deeper into spiritual practices but cannot find a way to make it happen without feeling trapped by some long-term, unalterable plan may find your way to a more joyful connection with God in some of the ideas that follow. Let "this counts" apply to more than you think is possible. There isn't just one way to be with God. To get you started, we offer a few practices here and even more in appendix A. Maybe some of these ideas will be for you the breadcrumbs of desire you need to enliven your soul on the pathway of joy.

Look at the birds. Sit quietly for five minutes with no agenda. Sometimes, I am inspired to sit in our backyard and watch the birds hop through our grass, looking for a spare crumb or sipping a few drops of leftover water from our sprinkler heads. And almost every time, these words pop into my head: "Look at the birds." These were words spoken by Jesus to a group of people as he taught them not to worry so much. *The Message* puts it this way: "Look at the birds, free and unfettered, not tied down to a job description, careless in the care of God. And you count far more to him than birds" (Matthew 6:26). You will be surprised by the clarity that may arise in that amount of time. Whether you are at home or on a break at the office, you can think back through the morning, maybe encounter a little peace, and then adjust how you want to live the rest of your day—from the inside out.

Notice grace. This is a great practice for the end of your day. If you type your thanks into your computer, be sure to slow down and become thoughtful. If you hand write your thanks, purchase a beautiful journal especially for gratitude. Let your mind wander back through your day and thank God for as many things as you can remember. Usually the big events come to mind first, but if you linger a bit, the small, mundane encounters sneak in. These are the hidden jewels of your day. Gratitude is one of the best ways to redirect your heart and your thoughts. It is a natural attitude shifter and the first step on the path to contentment.

Be intentional with your screensaver. I have actually used my computer screensaver to depict visually the current season of my soul. In this way, I've been able to access a bit of soul work in the day-to-day events of work.

When I was in a dark night, I used a black and white image of a pier jutting out over the water in the fog. It was so beautifully brooding. It was a wordless prayer every time I saw it. When I was in a season of waiting for something new to release from within me, I used the image of the inside of a desert cave. It was a swirling image full of gorgeous pinks, purples, and oranges. The point of view from the inside looking out wonderfully depicted my view before the birth of something new. After entering that next new place, I chose a beautiful pink lotus in full blossom as an image of new life and a new way of being in beauty, fullness, and growth.

When we began Unhurried Living, I was drawn to an airplane view of well-tended fields, each surrounded by a watering system. Each plot was delineated, cared for, and lush. It symbolized my newfound productivity, with rhythms and patterns in place and well-defined boundaries. And, as I write this, my desktop image is a splash of color and texture with stacks of shapes that create a fluid movement. It symbolizes the beautiful multiplicity of my life and work and brings me joy as I continue to do what I love to do.

I only realized I was choosing these perfectly metaphorical images after the fact. I didn't plan these screensavers in the full knowledge of where I was. I simply realized afterward that I had unconsciously chosen the images in each of these various seasons. My deepest heart knew where I was, and I was drawn to those images for a reason. And the images became a wordless prayer every time I opened my computer.

THE ENERGIZING JOY OF GOD

Andrew Murray offers some gentle and wise advice for those of us who are hungry to live in the energizing joy of God as we make our transforming journey. "You forget again; and instead of beginning each morning with the joyous transference of all the needs and cares of your spiritual life to the Father's charge, you again feel anxious, and burdened, and helpless. Is it not, perhaps, my friend, because you have not committed to the Father's care this matter of daily remembering to renew your entire surrender?"[2]

Why not offer this prayer? "Father, I see my need to grow more confident in your joyful care for me, to entrust myself more and more completely to your faithful care. Awaken me more and more to the reality of the safe and abundant kingdom in which I live my life and do my work. May joy like this energize and strengthen me. Today, yet again, I gratefully and joyfully acknowledge you, your leadership, and your way for me. Amen."

BE TRANSFORMED

1. In what ways do you resonate with the contrast of the pasture versus the maze idea?

2. In what ways have things turned out for you worse than you would have hoped? How has this made you feel about God's favor (or apparent lack thereof)?

3. If you were to write your own version of the Habakkuk passage, what failures, losses, or shortfalls might you mention beginning with the word *though*? How would you then voice your *yet* of joy, trust, peace, confidence? You might want to give writing out the passage a try!

4. How can you develop more of a sense of "this counts"?

5. Turn to appendix A for the full list of practices. Is there one from this chapter or from the appendix that you'd like to try?

time reading / relaxing
or doing nothing

–time to savor

10
PROCESS

STAYING ON THE PATH OF CHANGE

Unfolding—*This is synonymous with blooming. It is the slow, beautiful process of some area of your life opening up. It may be a time of moving from bud to flower. Tread gently during that time. Enjoy the blossoming of newness. Don't rush past. Use this word to engage in the overarching story of your life.*

STAYING ON THE PATH of being transformed more and more into the inviting image of Christ is not easy, but it is fruitful. I (Alan) have sometimes had a bad habit of avoiding hard things, but what truly good thing doesn't involve significant effort or training? The writer of Hebrews put it this way: "No discipline seems pleasant at the time, but painful. Later on, however, it produces a harvest of righteousness and peace for those who have been trained by it" (Hebrews 12:11).

Something in me rises up in reaction to a word like *discipline*. It feels like a synonym for punishment, but it's not that. It's training. Being trained by discipline is an experience of personal guidance from the Master Trainer. He is a perfect model for the transformation I hunger for. The pain in the moment of training is producing a harvest of something good and right. It is leading me to a life of peace and well-being.

It has been helpful to remember that the One who is training me knows me well and seeks my good. We might seek out a physical trainer if we'd like to be in better physical health and wholeness. How much more might we seek out the One who would train us for soul health and wholeness, the One who would lead us in the peaceful, wholesome way of transformation?

I'm sorry to say, though, that I have fallen into the temptation at times to settle for a faith and spiritual life defined mostly in terms of having the right answers to important doctrinal questions and doing things right (or at least looking that way to others). But the remarkable invitation of Jesus is to change that begins within us and is expressed more and more in our words, our manner, our way of relating to others and doing our work. We can actually become the sort of people from whom good words and good deeds more naturally flow. We can become gentle and humble in heart like Jesus is. We can become courageous and bold like Jesus is. We can become wise and kind in the spirit of Jesus. We can become beautiful with the beauty of God's heavenly home.

I am an imperfect traveler in my own spiritual journey. That is not a revelation. We are all imperfect travelers. As a recovering perfectionist, I have too often tried to *look* perfect, but that has always been about putting on a show rather than

living my actual life. Sometimes I have avoided our eight
transforming questions because they seemed too scary or too
hard. But whenever I have leaned into one of these questions,
I have discovered that I'm never alone there. I have been invited to come and follow Jesus in this journey. He knows my
need for change, even my desire for it, and is a wonderful
counselor and a wise guide. I needn't be afraid because I'm not
alone. I needn't worry about whether or not I can make it because I have good help.

I think of the invitation of Jesus to his first followers to "Come,
follow me," and, in the language of our eight questions, I wonder
if it might not sound like this for me:

Follow me. Let me help you experience the fuller reality of
my kingdom (truth). You needn't be afraid because you've
never been alone on this journey (fear). You might find a no
rising up from within you even as you intend to say yes to
me. I can help you discern the guiding voice of the Spirit
(resistance). It is safe to fully open your thoughts, your emotions, your intentions to me. I already know what you may
be timid to reveal. Let's look at it all together (vulnerability).

I know what you want and what you *think* you want. I
want to fulfill your truest, deepest longings in ways you
couldn't begin to imagine (desire). You will find lasting
energy for the journey as you come to more fully realize
how much pleasure I take in you and in all creation (joy).
You can lean into what hurts and find a fruitful way forward.
Wouldn't you prefer the pain of training to the pain of consequences (pain)? You can trust that I am watching over
you and release your white-knuckle grip on things (control).

In whatever way we might feel stuck on our path of transformation, we are not alone there. We have a Master Guide to show us our way forward.

Remember that you and I aren't the only persons walking the path of transformation. We are part of an ages-old and worldwide community of Christ followers. One of the great gifts in this is having others who can see with greater objectivity what we are too near to see with perspective. We can take the risk to open up about places where we feel on a plateau or at a dead-end. We can help one another not by first suggesting turn-by-turn directions for the next leg of the journey but by offering a compassionate and listening ear. It's amazing how often we find our own way to getting unstuck with the help of a friend who is willing to offer the gift of their attentive presence. Helping one another discern and follow the guidance of our heavenly mentor is a rich, encouraging opportunity.

> We were made to live in trusting relationships in which we help one another make our way.

There may be moments when we need more skilled help to continue on the fruitfully transforming way of Jesus. We have both benefitted from professional counseling and spiritual direction all along the way. The Spirit of God has used men and women who listened with compassion and responded in wisdom to what we shared. We've found our way to getting unstuck and finding healing and wholeness. You can too.

I say all of this knowing that I still find myself in familiar "I can do it myself" modes. It's not a healthy and holy independence, but a small and unholy isolation in which I become trapped. Rather than the mature voice of responsibility and fruitful action, it's the childish declaration of self-sufficient sovereignty. We were made to live in interdependent community. We were made to live in trusting relationships in which we help one another make our way.

Another way in which this transforming journey is communal is that we aren't being transformed only for our own good. The process isn't merely a personal improvement project. We aren't just seeking our own joy or peace. We are being transformed for the good of others. God invites Abraham to a life of blessing not just so he can be blessed, but so that he might have the capacity to bless others. "I will make you into a great nation, and I will bless you; I will make your name great, and you will be a blessing" (Genesis 12:2). He will be blessed beyond his ability to imagine, and he will be enabled to be a blessing beyond what he thought possible. Being blessed and being a blessing are key intentions of God in our transformation.

We are transformed so that we can live as salt and light in our world. We are meant to bring out the inviting flavor of this good world God has made (salt). We are meant to shine graciously and gently on the good paths to which God is inviting each one (light).

Rather than moralizing about what's right and wrong, we might find ourselves living more and more wholesome and gracious lives. From such abundance, we can invite others into the goodness of living in friendship with Jesus.

> Being blessed and being a blessing are key intentions of God in our transformation.

Rather than shining a self-righteous spotlight at wrongs we perceive in the lives of others, we can glow with the inviting and healing light of God. Our lives can become good news to others, even as we bear witness to the good news of traveling this journey with Jesus.

Spiritual transformation is not just a theoretical good. It has been good for our relationships, good for our emotional well-being, good for our vocational fruitfulness, good in so many ways. For example, when it comes to anger, there was a time early in our marriage in which I (Alan) could easily lose my temper. I would always be sorry and sad for my bad behavior, but I'd continue to return to such places in seasons of great stress or weariness. But when I began to walk in the light of sharing my story with a trusted counselor, the deep anger that I too often tapped into began to dissipate. It was transformed into mercy and understanding. This healing seemed to drain the anger I had too often tapped into in the past. I am so grateful for ways that gentleness and patience are a bit

> We are not junk needing to be radically repurposed. We are masterpieces needing to be restored. Original goodness precedes original sin.

more natural for me now than they used to be. Transformation is our inheritance as children of God. We are being trained to live well and lead well in the kingdom of our heavenly Father.

You can probably think of some ways in which you have tasted and enjoyed the good fruit of God's transforming work in your life. Being transformed as a creative expression of the divine artist is such an honor. We are called "God's handiwork, created in Christ Jesus to do good works, which God prepared in advance for us to do" (Ephesians 2:10). We are not junk needing to be radically repurposed. We are masterpieces needing to be restored. Original goodness precedes original sin.

A POSTURE FOR TRANSFORMATION

We've gathered together here some elements we introduced throughout the book. Our own cooperative process plays a role in allowing growth to occur. Having this posture toward life can keep us moving when we get stuck or are uncertain of the way forward. It is a posture we can take toward God and our own lives to remain pliable as he brings us to maturity, in his will and in his way.

Open: Do you want it? Ask yourself if you are open. Do you want to be fully formed into the image of Christ? On the surface, this is an easy question. Of course, you want this. But since we are talking about the process of transformation and all of the dynamics we addressed in this book, it might be good to check in once again to be sure. Ensure that you are not a closed system. Are you willing to entertain the idea that you do not know everything? If you have lingering doubts as to whether or not you really want to be transformed, you may unknowingly become your own resistance. Being open as a first step may look like opening the door of your heart and letting God know that you are ready to welcome him into every room so you can get a good look at everything together. In *New Seeds of Contemplation*, Thomas Merton writes,

> Every moment and every event of a person's life on earth plants something good in their soul. For just as the wind carries thousands of winged seeds, so each moment brings with it germs of spiritual vitality that come to rest imperceptibly in the minds and wills of people. Most of these unnumbered seeds perish and are lost, because people are not prepared to receive them: for such seeds as these cannot spring up anywhere except in the good soil of freedom, spontaneity and love.[1]

So, are you open? Are you prepared to receive whatever God is bringing to you?

Aware: Are you noticing? Once you've determined that you are open to all God has for you in your transformational journey, you can grow in becoming more aware. Awareness means your eyes are open and you begin to notice what's going on inside of you. You pay attention to your patterns, habits, longings, and desires. You can also notice what is going on around you and what your natural reactions are in any given situation. Notice your resistances. Notice when you are bugged. Notice when you are at peace. Awareness is key because you cannot change what you do not see.

Awareness takes work because the culture around us does not encourage it. The pace of our lives as well as the tendency to numb, deny, or distract move us away from presence. And presence is one of the keys to awareness. Like any good, loving virtue, presence takes time, which means awareness takes time. This continues to be the centerpiece of what we do at Unhurried Living. We remind people in multiple and various ways that we are addressing the inside hurry. The outer circumstances of our lives may continue to be busy, but we do have a say about our inner lives. And that is where hurry resides. So we talk about slowing inside, and this includes presence and awareness. Where will we set our eyes? Colossians 3 gives us a hint:

> So if you're serious about living this new resurrection life with Christ, *act* like it. Pursue the things over which Christ presides. Don't shuffle along, eyes to the ground, absorbed with the things right in front of you. Look up, and be alert to what is going on around Christ—that's where the action is. See things from *his* perspective.
>
> Your old life is dead. Your new life, which is your *real* life—even though invisible to spectators—is with Christ in

God. *He* is your life. When Christ (your real life, remember)
shows up again on this earth, you'll show up, too—the real
you, the glorious you. (Colossians 3:1-4 *The Message*)

There is no way around this. Just as love doesn't happen at
breakneck pace, neither does transformation. Finding a way to
slow down enough inside to become aware of what is going on
is key to change and growth.

Willing: Are you willing to take action? Once you start becoming aware of your inner dynamics, it's time to ask yourself if
you are willing to engage in the groundwork of change. Are you
willing to act? Willing means you are determined to take steps
forward in your process. It may be a small step, but you are still
willing to take it. Sometimes you have to acknowledge that you
aren't quite willing yet. In that case it's perfectly okay to back up
a bit and say, "I am willing to be willing." It may seem like a
mind game or simple semantics, but saying that you are willing
to be willing is a viable way to take your next step toward what
you desire.

Fear, control, pain, or resistance may get in the way. Alterna-
tively, you may be propelled forward by desire, vulnerability, truth,
or joy. For most of us, willingness kicks in when the pain of staying
where we are becomes greater than the fear of moving forward. At
that point, it feels like we have no choice but to reach out.

Whatever your motivation, confirming that you are willing to
act is part of the ongoing process of moving forward in transformation. Like most processes, *open, aware, and willing* is cyclical
and not always linear. You may have this trio humming along
nicely in one area while in another area you haven't yet found
a way to be open. All of this is normal. We are multi-faceted,
complicated beings. To keep yourself from being overwhelmed,

remember to be kind to yourself, watch out for the inner critic, and simply take the next step forward that you can see, at the pace of grace.

ENGAGING TRANSFORMATION

The process of *open, aware, and willing* works as an overarching paradigm for how you can move through your life open to transformation. You can also track the movement within a specific area of your life. As a very real-life example, I have been working on my physical health for quite a number of years. I have endured many fits, starts, and setbacks, but I have been determined not to give up. I have continued to move forward in my own imperfect way. I've grown open and aware, but my willingness keeps ebbing and flowing.

However, some recent blood tests showed that my blood glucose and cholesterol numbers are rising. And my weight was climbing at an unacceptable rate, stealing my energy and vitality. A decision was in front of me. Do I keep trying and failing, or do I try to make a lifestyle change that takes into account the reality of my physical health?

The seriousness of my situation helped me decide that I really wanted to change. So I then determined that I was, again, *willing* to spend some time listening to and cooperating with God as he unpacked my issue with food and exercise. What do I do next?

Being open, aware, and willing can work for any level of healing or growth. In the garden of our souls, our eyes can be open, we can become aware, and we can grow in our willingness to continue the process. We've set the heart stage, and we are ready for action. But instead of turning this into a to-do list, we're going to keep these actions relational and process oriented.

And we'll look at how the example of dealing with my health can flow through the rest of this process.

Invitation: What is God's invitation to you? The word *invitation* has a way of taking the duty out of the action. Every time you receive an invitation in the mail it has been lovingly sent by someone who desires your presence. The word *invitation* can take the edge off of our to-do list. With God, we don't have to bear up under the weight of our inner or outer work. If you ask yourself, *What is God inviting me to these days?* it becomes possible to move your mind and heart to the level of the divine breathings. Instead of imagining God as an unbending coach with a clipboard, *invitation* can bring to mind Jesus as the Good Shepherd. We can hear him say, "Come to me" and "Come follow me." Our actions are then tied to relationship. As we continue to remember that God is inviting us into continual relationship, our growth and our actions can become less burdensome.

Returning to my example of becoming healthy, an invitation from God might look like this: *Gem, I know that you have been able to do as you please with food for most of your life and not suffer any consequences. However, you are now at an age where you'll have to work a little harder to remain healthy. I invite you to step into a new way of thinking about food. I have given it to you for nutrition and sustenance. Let's address together your usual mode of comfort eating. I invite you to look to me for satisfaction, filling, and wholeness.*

See how looking at food and health from the vantage point of invitation is, well, more invitational? I have trained myself to listen well to God in solitude and silence so that I can notice his invitations in various circumstances. I can more easily open this invitation because there is no condemnation in it. I see words and phrases like "I invite you," "I have given you," "Let's address this together," and "Look to me." This is how the Spirit of God speaks to us as we seek transformation. God knows our hearts. If you are hearing judgment or condemnation, it might be good to discern whose voice that is. Maybe it's an old inner recording of one of your parents, your own inner critic, or it might even be the enemy of your soul.

Intention: What is the yes you want to say? Once you've decided to receive God's gift of invitation, you can move toward intention. What is the yes you want to say? Again, resisting the temptation to take your invitation and create yet another to-do list, seek to keep this real and relational, which means it needs to come from somewhere inside of you.

External pressure only works for so long, and then we can easily give up under the weight of duty yet again. An intention usually involves being in touch with some level of desire, and we know that desire bubbles up from the question, What do you want?

In my example of dealing with my health, my intention had to come from deep within me. I am in one of the most vibrant seasons of my life. I'm building a non-profit with my husband. We are training, speaking, and producing content. How does my yes emerge from this? My yes is that I want to be able to physically keep up with the vitality I am experiencing in my life and work. I want that more than I want Cheetos and sour cream and a donut. I intend to trust God and give thanks for every part of the process, and I intend to remember that God is with me.

The relational part of my intention is intact. I connect my wants and desires to God's invitation. Intentions are not a one-time fix. I have to remind myself multiple times that this is what I want. I may have built a strong pattern, and it will take some time to change that habit. And I can still practice in the meantime. I want to keep moving. I don't want to get stuck. I intend to remember that God is with me and that I desire to be vital and healthy. We can strive for patterns over perfection. It is taking me years to change my patterns, but my heart is being transformed the entire time I engage my invitations and intentions. That is how I get closer to my desired change.

Response: How do you want to proceed? Now that we have our invitation in mind and our intention in heart, how do we respond? What can you actually do in response to your invitation? Again, it can be tempting to think that this is a simple 1-2-3 process. Done. But at this point in our conversation I think we can all agree that transformation takes time and is a journey with many ups and downs. So there is no need for herculean moves here. It is best to start small, simple, and gracious.

In response to my health issue, this is what I am doing as of this writing. I've already tried all the diets and gym memberships, and I have educated myself about nutritional foods. What I'm missing is encouragement and accountability. So I signed up for one year of group coaching. It came with workout videos, lessons on nutrition, a coach, and an app to be in touch with other women who are on the same journey as me.

These are the changes I've enacted: I exercise thirty minutes a day, five days a week (in my own living room). I touch base with my team daily, and we give each other virtual high fives on our progress. And I have a new way of looking at food thanks to this program and food writer Michael Pollan. He writes, "Eat food. Not too much. Mostly plants."[2] I have also found that the one-word prayer *today* has saved me and kept me moving. Not "for the rest of my life," but "today."

THE HUMBLE WAY OF TRANSFORMATION

If we are going to remain on the path of transformation, it helps
if we keep things small, simple, and gracious. Multiple small
moves strung together create lasting change. One huge move
that boomerangs back on us can be discouraging and disheart-
ening. Let's see if my response passes the small, simple, and
gracious test.

Small. For me, the herculean move would have been another
gym membership and another diet. Instead, I opted for something smaller: thirty minutes a day in my own home. There is
less resistance when all I have to do is walk downstairs and turn
on the TV. And instead of another diet, I simply eat real food
(focus on *real*) and mostly plants.

Simple. The simple part leaps out at me from Michael Pollan's
counsel: "Eat food. Not too much. Mostly plants." I understand
this, and I can actually do it. By "eat food" he means real, not
packaged. There is nothing fancy about this, and I can maintain
this for a long time.

Gracious. The *today* prayer is the graciousness of this response. When I became overwhelmed with thinking about doing
this "for the rest of my life," I wanted to quit. But God offered
me this one-word prayer. Today I choose to eat like this. Today
I choose to exercise. Today I choose health.

I remind myself that I am doing the best I can with the
knowledge and abilities I currently have. I have kept my inner
critic subdued, and I assure myself that I am continuing in my
process. Grace is like oil that keeps the gears moving. Condemnation and criticism can cause my gears to grind. Keeping it
gracious means that I can continue trying over and over until I
am changed from the inside out.

OPEN OR CLOSED

EXERCISE

This interactive exercise can offer you an expansive vision of God's presence as you make your way forward. Put your arms out in front of you and touch your fingers together to form a circle (as if you were holding a large, round ball).

Now, look down into that space.

Many of us unconsciously think everything that is a possibility will fit right there in that space. We think we have access only to what we can wrap our arms or our minds around. It is a relatively small space. Would you agree?

In the book of Colossians, Paul is writing to a group of people who thought that Jesus was merely a great person among many other great ones. He writes to encourage the Colossians to move Jesus to the center. Jesus is without peers. He describes Jesus to them, as well as their place in reference to him, saying, "For in Christ all the fullness of the Deity lives in bodily form, and in Christ you have been brought to fullness" (Colossians 2:9-10).

Now, get ready for some wise words from author and Anglican Bishop, Todd Hunter: "You are not living in a system that is limited to what you think you presently have."[3]

Read that sentence again. Let it sink in.

Now, open your arms wide out to your side, as if you were standing on top of a mountain, sun on your face, breeze blowing through your hair. Take a deep breath and read: "For in Christ all the fullness of the Deity lives in bodily form, and in Christ you have been brought to fullness."

On the journey of transformation it is good to have an "arms open" stance. Fullness looks more like arms wide than arms closed. You have more than you think you do. So much so, in fact, that you could not wrap your arms around it. This is the truth.

When you hit a bump in the road in one of your friendships and you are misunderstood and belittled—*In Christ, you have been brought to fullness.*

When you need to have a difficult conversation with a board member—*In Christ, you have been brought to fullness.*

When you find out that you are giving a presentation at work and speaking to groups terrifies you—*In Christ, you have been brought to fullness.*

When you are hunched over a baby, changing the twelfth diaper of the day and your toddler is screaming and pulling on your leg—*In Christ, you have been brought to fullness.*

As you study for the final exam for a class in which you struggle—*In Christ, you have been brought to fullness.*

"So if you're serious about living this new resurrection life with Christ, *act* like it. Pursue the things over which Christ presides. Don't shuffle along, eyes to the ground, absorbed with the things right in front of you. Look up, and be alert to what is going on around Christ—that's where the action is. See things from *his* perspective.

"Your old life is dead. Your new life, which is your *real* life—even though invisible to spectators—is with Christ in God. *He* is your life" (Colossians 3:1-3 *The Message*).

As you continue on in your life of transformation in the way of these eight questions and others, our hope is that you gain a vision for making your way forward with not only arms open but also mind and heart. It is our real lives, our day-to-day activities that invite us to engage with this truth. *In Christ, you have been brought to fullness.*

BE TRANSFORMED

1. What are some ways in which you desire to continue on in your journey of transformation?

2. What are some ways in which you can see that your own transformation will benefit those around you?

3. What are a few of your favorite process words? How might you begin to use them to keep moving forward?

4. How will an "arms open" stance in your life help you? How might it bring encouragement in your relationships?

- take time to breathe + relax
- more harmony in relationships
- be kinder

ACKNOWLEDGMENTS

FROM THE BEGINNING, as we worked on this book, we often needed places to get away to focus our attention. Thank you, Grace and Steve Cabalka, for the use of your Avila Beach condo, Villa Risa, and your studio downstairs. Thank you, too, Dave and Cathy Huseby, for offering time at your remote cabin near Duck Creek Village, Utah. Both locations provided us a remote home for the intensive planning, composing, and revising of this book.

For the InterVarsity Press team. It is our privilege to work with such a stellar group of people. We give thanks for you often. Jeff Crosby, thank you for your constant encouragement. Cindy Bunch, you are a skilled spiritual director to authors and their book projects. Lori Neff, your enthusiasm always makes us feel encouraged and welcomed. Andrew Bronson, thank you for your wisdom and connections. Alisse Wissman, Helen Lee, and Krista Clayton, thank you for all of the ways you support this project. And thank you to the rest of the IVP team.

For David Fassett, who designed our book cover. We've been impressed with your work for a while and we are grateful for the beautiful cover you created for us.

For my (Gem's) dear friends, Marla Christian, Stacey Green, Kristi Gaultiere, Kristi DeVito, Nancy Lopez, and Shaleen Camery-Hoggatt. All six of you have held my heart at various points along this writing journey. You listened as I processed my joys and my fears. Thank you from the bottom of my heart.

And for our friends Tom and Marla Christian. You have walked with us for ten years now, through the thick of our journey in life and ministry. Thank you for being such gracious listeners and kind friends.

I (Alan) want to thank Stephen Macchia and James Bryan Smith for some especially encouraging conversations, especially at the moment when we stepped out to launch Unhurried Living. I'm grateful for your encouraging, affirming presence in my life.

To our legal and advisory board members, Dave and Cathy Huseby, Tom and Marla Christian, Jeff and Mary Linam, Jeb Shore, and Darrell Warner: thank you for standing with us as we have navigated our way through the various challenges and opportunities of building Unhurried Living. You have been encouragers and partners with us, especially in the process of completing this book.

Thank you to our Unhurried Living ministry team: Matt Fogle, Kara Yuza, and Belinda Kent. Each one of you is a gift God has given us along the way. Our initial connections with each of you were a unique and creative expression of God's grace to us. Thank you for the way you continue to walk with us and partner with us in this work.

For Holy Trinity Anglican Church in Costa Mesa, and our bishop, Todd Hunter. You have been a supportive community and a wonderful home for our souls' journey.

And finally, to our Unhurried Living community—donors, pray-ers, readers, podcast listeners, event-attenders, email recipients—many of you listened to us talk about this material as we wrote and gave us helpful and encouraging feedback. We especially thank our inner circle of 160 friends who prayed often as this book was coming together. To each one who said, "I need this book now," here it is. We offer it with our love and gratitude.

CREATIVE SPIRITUAL PRACTICES

W HAT DOES YOUR SOUL LOVE? What follows are some ideas of spiritual practices that might help you find a more joyful connection with God. There isn't just one way to be with God. These ideas "count" as spiritual exercises. Maybe some of these ideas will be for you the breadcrumbs of desire you need to enliven your soul on the pathway of joy.

Get out in nature. Forest bathing is a newer trend, and studies have shown that it can help to reduce blood pressure and certain stress hormones. That's great news, but even better is that nature is one of the easiest ways to enjoy the presence of God. The psalms are full of references to mountains, trees, oceans, flora, and fauna all crying out the grandeur of God. "From the beginning, creation in its magnificence enlightens us to His nature. Creation itself makes His undying power and divine identity clear" (Romans 1:20 *The Voice*).

This one may take a bit of planning if you want to enter a real forest. But even if you live in a city there are ways to enjoy some greenery, a park, or an arboretum. Let yourself stroll. Breathe deeply. This counts in a big way.

ASBC journal. A, S, B, and *C* are the initials of my (Gem) husband and three sons. I have a special handmade, leather-bound journal for my guys. This is where I write a one-sentence prayer for each of them. One sentence. I keep it short because I want to distill the essence of my greatest anxieties or my greatest longings for them in that moment. I usually end up with a sense of peace when I write in this because my requests are so central to who they are, and I know that I can trust them into God's care.

Spiritual reading. Like many of you, I usually have a few good books going at any one time. I move from one to another at will. It does not work for me to choose one book and read it all the way through. I give myself permission not to start at the beginning or to not even finish the book. To those of you who are disciplined rule followers, this may sound like anathema. But it is what keeps me going. If I make unbending rules for myself, my natural inclination is to break them. Then a million becomes zero, and I end up with nothing. With spiritual reading, it is important that it be truly soul filling. It is not a race. Take it in at a pace that matches your own growth. If you aren't connecting with the writer or the content, it is okay to set the book down for a bit. I've done that before, only to find out I was ready later on to pick it back up and finish.

Take a stroll. Make your way to some place beautiful. Or simply walk out your front door. Walk slowly. Breathe deeply. Meander a bit. You aren't walking for aerobic exercise when you stroll. Let go of your to-do list and let your mind wander over the past day or week. Reflect on your current season of life. Take note of any tension physically or emotionally. See what meaning may emerge as you slow the pace of your body. Cast your cares on God and receive God's invitation to slowing.

Find a chapel. Find a church or retreat center in your area that has a beautiful chapel or sanctuary. Many modern churches meet in uninspiring business-park buildings. However, there are still a few churches and retreat centers built a few years ago that have some old-world charm and maybe even a stained-glass window or two. If you can locate one near you, ask permission to go there mid-week and pray. Enjoy the silence of the empty chapel. Gaze at the cross. If there are art pieces, enjoy them and let their beauty open you up to even more reflection.

Listen to worship music. Listen to a worship song. Sometimes, I will scroll through my "Christian" playlist until a song strikes me. Other times, a song will come to mind, and I will go directly to it. When that happens, I find that the Spirit prompts exactly what my soul needs. Sometimes I've played the song on repeat, and it has become a heartfelt prayer. The words and the music give voice to a prayer I had yet to pray.

Visit a museum. Museums are full of beautiful paintings and sculptures, and often have lush, manicured gardens. Plan a day or half day and really take in the beauty. Let your mind wander as you stroll the grounds. Let an image or sculpture capture your imagination. Notice the thoughts and feelings that emerge. See if any of the art speaks to something going on in your life right now. Art has a way of tapping into your soul in different ways than words. Let yourself be moved by the artist's rendering of people and scenery. Interact with God about what emerges.

Practice listening prayer. This can happen anywhere, anytime, and for any length of time. Instead of bombarding God with many words, simply stop, get quiet, and listen for a bit. You may want to let God know your intention: *God, I want to stop and reflect for just a bit. Would you please help me slow down? Would you please bring up anything you want me to see? I trust you.*

Share with a friend. I have a very small group of friends with whom I can share my life. Not only the regular moments, but the deep, behind-the-scenes thoughts and feelings I am having. These are the kinds of friends who know how to listen and care without moving to problem solving. Their listening, their empathy, and their solid love for me make me feel safe. God meets me in these friendships. Having another trusted person to listen is a wonderful way to reflect on your life, and it is a gift directly from the hand of God.

Listen to Scripture. My favorite way to "read" the Bible is actually to listen to it. I have *The Message* version of the New Testament as a playlist on my phone. Scripture comes alive in a different way when you listen to a chapter or two unbroken by paragraphs and verse numbers. Getting a feel for more of the sweeping narrative can help you take in the words with more than your mind. Very often I will notice the nuance in what is being said in a way I did not by reading it on paper. Meet God with your "heart ears." It might be a way to enliven the Bible for you in a drier season.

Pray by name. Like many, I have a list of people I pray for. Sometimes the list feels overwhelming. There are so many people and so many needs. When I am tempted not to pray due to the sheer volume, I simply read each name out loud slowly. I let God know my intention at the start. I am giving each person to him, knowing that he knows and loves them perfectly. I read their names in God's presence and I trust him. This is a very peaceful way to pray.

Journaling. I have a love/hate relationship with journaling. I love getting my ideas down for posterity. But I also don't like engaging my thoughts in such a linear way. Once I start typing, at times, the feeling of connection to what I am sharing goes away because the computer can feel too detached. So sometimes I get out my journal and a pen and engage my thoughts that way. The beauty of the written word is that it slows you down, and there is something more elegant about the swirl of the pen stroke on the paper. Either way, journaling is a wonderful way to connect with your thoughts. You can read them over and see if something new emerges that you couldn't see before because it was a flurry swirling around your brain.

A PROCESS FOR TRANSFORMATION

Below is an overview of the process for transformation mentioned in the final chapter. What follows is the posture, the engagement, and the manner in which you can keep moving along the path of transformation.

THE POSTURE OF TRANSFORMATION

Open: Do you want it? Ask yourself how open you are to being transformed. Do you want to be fully formed into the image of Christ? It's good to ensure that your life is not a closed system. Are you willing to entertain the idea that you do not know everything? Are you prepared to receive whatever God is bringing to you?

Aware: Are you noticing? Awareness means your eyes are open and you are noticing what's going on inside of you. You continue to pay attention to your patterns, habits, longings, and desires. You can also stay awake to what is going on around you and what your natural reactions are in any given situation. Notice your resistances. Notice when you are bugged. Notice when you are at peace. Awareness is key because you cannot change what you do not see.

Willing: Are you willing to take action? Are you willing to act? "Willing" means you are determined to take steps forward in your process. It may be a simple and small step, but you are still willing to take it. For most of us, willingness kicks in when the pain of staying where we are becomes greater than the fear of moving forward. Whatever your motivation, confirming that you are willing to act is part of the process of moving forward in transformation.

ENGAGING TRANSFORMATION

Invitation: What is God's invitation to you? The word *invitation* has a way of removing a sense of obligation from the action we take. It can cause our to-do list to feel less overwhelming. *Invitation* can bring to mind Jesus as the Good Shepherd. As we continue to remember that God is inviting us into continual relationship, our growth and our actions can become less burdensome.

Intention: What is the yes you want to say? We seek to keep this process real and relational, which means it needs to come from somewhere inside of us. An intention usually involves being in touch with some level of desire, and desire bubbles up from the question "What do you want?" We connect our wants and desires to God's invitation. We want to keep moving and not get stuck. We remember that God is with us and we strive for patterns over perfection.

Response: How do you want to proceed? How do we respond? What can you actually do in response to God's invitation and your intention? Instead of being tied to an ill-fitting to-do list, our response can flow naturally from our intention, which flows naturally from God's invitation. This method of engagement keeps relationship with God at the center and our connection to him imperative.

THE HUMBLE WAY OF TRANSFORMATION

Herculean moves have a way of causing a boomerang effect. The tension of maintaining something so large can backfire. If we are going to remain on the path of transformation, it helps if we keep things small, simple, and gracious.

Small. How small can you make your next step of growth? It's okay to let it be ridiculously small. The smaller the better. One minute of this. Five minutes of that. That way you can get the habit forming. It's the habit that will result in lasting change. Once the habit is in place, you can add more time and further engagement.

Simple. Simplicity means it is not complicated. You could describe it to a third grader and they would know exactly what you mean. Extravagant plans seldom last for the long haul. Keeping it simple means that there is nothing fancy about this and I can do this for a long time. We're looking for profound simplicity.

Gracious. I remind myself that I am doing the best I can with the knowledge and abilities I currently have. I have kept my inner critic subdued and I assure myself that I am continuing in my process. Grace is like oil that keeps the gears moving. Condemnation and criticism can have a brake-pedal effect. Keeping it gracious means that I can keep trying over and over until I am changed from the inside out.

APPENDIX C

GROUP GUIDE

THE GUIDE BELOW IS DESIGNED for a five-session small group or a leadership experience. Each week, participants will read two chapters and spend a little time with the end-of-chapter "Be Transformed" questions, process words, and exercises in preparation for the group meeting and interaction. This guide assumes about one hour spent together with the material.

This guide is not so much a "study guide" as it is a guide for a shared soul care experience. In groups like this it is good to remember to walk alongside one another. Resist the desire to fix or give answers. Listen to and hold onto each other's stories and answers with honor and respect. Be ready to share as openly and honestly as you are able. And agree that what is shared will stay within the relationships of the group.

Group Preparation for Meeting One

Read chapters one and two.

Reflect on the end-of-chapter questions for those chapters.

Experiment with the chapter two exercise.

Meeting One

Reflect together on the questions from chapters one and two. Some questions invite conversation. Some invite a moment of praying as a group. Let the questions guide you in this.

Discuss the process word *slow*. What about that word is attractive? What about that word provokes resistance in you?

How might you slow down *inside* in a world that's going so fast on the *outside*?

The chapter two exercise is a reflection on the story of the bleeding woman who comes to Jesus (Luke 8:43-48). To the degree you feel secure to do so as a group, talk about ways you are hungry for God's healing or cleansing in your inner life, or how you're sometimes tempted to hide something of yourself from God or others.

Let question 4 from chapter two guide your closing prayer. Envision yourself as the paralytic being lowered into the presence of Jesus (Mark 2:1-12). What do you want Jesus to do for you? Offer that as a prayer in the midst of this supportive community.

Group Preparation for Meeting Two

Read chapters three and four.

Reflect on the end-of-chapter questions for those chapters.

Give attention to the three process words at the beginning of these chapters. Notice especially the ways in which the word *but* surfaces in everyday conversation. Does it make a difference to try the word *and* in some of those situations?

Meeting Two

Reflect together on the questions from chapters three and four.

Discuss the three process words for this week from these chapters: *seasons, and,* and *grace.* Which is the most inviting to you at this point in your journey? Which one provokes the most resistance? What do you think is the source of this resistance?

Try on the exercise in chapter four.

Let question 4 from chapter four become a closing prayer. Talk to God about how you want him to be a safe hiding place for you.

Group Preparation for Meeting Three

Read chapters five and six.

Reflect on the end-of-chapter questions for those chapters.

Give attention to the three process words at the beginning of these chapters. Try these words on in your thinking and even in your conversation.

Meeting Three

Reflect together on the questions from chapters five and six.

Discuss the three process words for this week from these chapters: *notice, discern,* and *acceptance*. Which of these three words feels the easiest for you to embrace? Which feels the most challenging? In what way do you find it challenging?

Try on the exercise in chapter five. Experiment with one member of your group as a volunteer answering the "three whys" described in that chapter.

It may be that real pain will have surfaced in the discussion of that chapter and those questions. Close your gathering with prayers for comfort or healing for one another.

Group Preparation for Meeting Four

Read chapters seven and eight.

Reflect on the end-of-chapter questions for these chapters.

Give attention to the three process words at the beginning of these chapters. Which seems the most helpful to you in this season of your life? Which is the hardest to connect with?

Meeting Four

Reflect together on the questions from chapters seven and eight.

Discuss the three process words for this week from these chapters: *with, mystery,* and *letting go*. Talk about which seems easiest for you to embrace and which feels the most challenging.

Try on the exercise in chapter seven. Discuss what might be in your backpack these days. What burdens are you carrying alone that you might carry together with Jesus?

The focus of this gathering has been on fear and control. Perhaps close with a prayer for God's love to displace fear in your lives, and for peace and inner confidence to displace the urge to take control.

Group Preparation for Meeting Five

Read chapters nine and ten.

Reflect on the end-of-chapter questions for these chapters.

Give attention to the three process words at the beginning of these chapters. Are you especially drawn to one of these? What most attracts you to this word? How might it become part of your thinking and speaking in the next few days?

Browse the practices in Appendix A. Is there one you'd like to experiment with and then share about in your next meeting? Give it a try.

Meeting Five

Reflect together on the questions from chapters nine and ten. (For question 5 in chapter nine, let anyone who experimented with one of the practices in Appendix A share about their experience.)

Discuss the three process words for this week from these chapters: *flow, unfolding,* and *process.* Share any of your reflections on them or experiences with them in reflection or conversation with others.

In this final meeting, talk about what has been most helpful over these five weeks. What changes in your thinking, your conversation, or your way of life have you noticed? What next step in your journey of transformation do you sense Jesus inviting you to?

Close with prayers of gratitude and of offering your intentions to continue this transforming journey with Jesus.

NOTES

1 INVITATION: CHANGING FROM THE CENTER

[1]Thomas Kelly, *A Testament of Devotion* (San Francisco: HarperSanFrancisco, 1941), 9.

[2]Kelly, *A Testament of Devotion*, 12-14.

2 DESIRE: WHAT DO YOU REALLY WANT?

[1]Jasmine Fox-Skelly, "What Does It Take to Live at the Bottom of the Ocean?" *BBC Earth*, January 29, 2015, www.bbc.com/earth/story/20150129-life-at-the-bottom-of-the-ocean.

[2]Fox-Skelly, "What Does It Take to Live at the Bottom of the Ocean?"

[3]Fox-Skelly, "What Does It Take to Live at the Bottom of the Ocean?"

[4]St. Augustine, *Letter to Proba*, letter 130:15. Translation found at www.crossroadsinitiative.com/media/articles/prayer-expands-desire.

3 RESISTANCE: WHAT IS GETTING IN YOUR WAY?

[1]Henri Nouwen, Michael J. Christensen, and Rebecca J. Laird, *Spiritual Direction* (San Francisco: HarperSanFrancisco, 2006), 98.

[2]Gerald May, *Simply Sane* (New York: Crossroads, 1993), 70-71.

[3]This is the first triad in a three-triad dynamic that is fully unpacked in the final chapter, "Process: Staying on the Path of Change."

4 VULNERABILITY: WHERE ARE YOU HIDING?

[1]David Benner, *Surrender to Love* (Downers Grove, IL: InterVarsity Press, 2015), 74.

[2]Brené Brown, *Daring Greatly: How the Courage to Be Vulnerable Transforms the Way We Live, Love, Parent, and Lead* (New York: Avery, 2015), 34.

[3]Thomas Merton, *No Man Is an Island* (New York: Harcourt Brace & Company, 1955), 168.

[4]Richard Rohr, "Vulnerability," Center for Action and Contemplation, September 27, 2016, https://cac.org/vulnerability-2016-09-27.

[5]David Bosch, *Spirituality of the Road* (Eugene, OR: Wipf & Stock, 2001), 76-77.

[6]Andy Crouch, *Strong and Weak* (Downers Grove, IL: InterVarsity Press, 2016), 12.

5 TRUTH: WHAT IS MOST REAL TO YOU?

[1]David Benner, *The Gift of Being Yourself* (Downers Grove, IL: InterVarsity Press, 2015), 53, 58.

[2]Alan Fadling, *An Unhurried Leader: The Lasting Fruit of Daily Influence* (Downers Grove, IL: InterVarsity Press, 2017), 67.

[3]This is the second triad in a three-triad dynamic that is fully unpacked in the final chapter, "Process: Staying on the Path of Change."

[4]Ricardo Semler, "How to Run a Company with (Almost) No Rules," Ted.com, October 2014, www.ted.com/talks/ricardo_semler_how_to_run_a_company_with_almost_no_rules#t-1046040.

[5]Paraphrased from a private conversation on September 10, 2014, with Dr. Ken Londeaux, Ed.D., ABMP, licensed psychologist.

6 PAIN: HOW ARE YOU SUFFERING?

[1]Tim Hughes, "Everything," *Holding Nothing Back*, Sparrow/Survivor, 2007.

[2]Frederick Buechner, *The Hungering Dark* (New York: HarperCollins, 1985), 14.

[3]Eugene Peterson, *The Old Testament Wisdom Books in Contemporary Language: The Message* (Colorado Springs: NavPress, 1996), 11-12.

[4]Peterson, *Old Testament Wisdom Books*, 11.

[5]Statistic from "Humanity's 100 Deadliest Achievements," www.bookof horriblethings.com/ax02.html. Accessed February 17, 2019.

[6]Anne Morrow Lindbergh, *Hour of Gold, Hour of Lead: Diaries and Letters of Anne Morrow Lindbergh, 1929-1932* (Wilmington, DE: Mariner Books, 1973), 3.

7 FEAR: WHAT ARE YOU AFRAID OF?

[1]Reginald Somerset Ward, *A Guide for Spiritual Directors* (London: A. R. Mowbray & Co., 1957), 19-20.

8 CONTROL: WHAT ARE YOU CLINGING TO?

[1]This story is a revised version of Gem Fadling, "A Choice That Can Reduce Anxiety," The Unhurried Living blog, July 13, 2015, https://unhurriedliving.com/blog/a-choice-that-reduces-anxiety.

[2]Jean-Pierre de Caussade, *Self-Abandonment to Divine Providence* (Rockford, IL: Tan Books, 1959), 5.

[3]de Caussade, *Self-Abandonment*, 8.

[4]de Caussade, *Self-Abandonment*, 12.

[5]Eugene Peterson, *The Jesus Way* (Grand Rapids: Eerdmans, 2007), 44.

[6]Dallas Willard, *Renovation of the Heart: Putting on the Character of Christ* (Colorado Springs: NavPress, 2002), 150-51.

[7]Dallas Willard, *The Divine Conspiracy* (New York: HarperCollins, 1998), 76.

[8]This is the final triad in a three-triad dynamic that is fully unpacked in the final chapter, "Process: Staying on the Path of Change."

9 JOY: WHAT DOES YOUR SOUL LOVE?

[1]Gem Fadling, "Love Well," The Unhurried Living blog, April 18, 2018, https://unhurriedliving.com/blog/love-well.

[2]Andrew Murray, *Abide in Christ* (Fort Washington, PA: Christian Literature Crusade, 1968), 74-75.

10 PROCESS: STAYING ON THE PATH OF CHANGE

[1]Thomas Merton, *New Seeds of Contemplation* (Boston: Shambala, 2003), 16.

[2]Michael Pollan, *In Defense of Food* (New York: Penguin, 2009).

[3]Todd D. Hunter, sermon given at Holy Trinity Anglican Church in Costa Mesa, California, January 4, 2015.

ALSO AVAILABLE

An Unhurried Leader
978-0-8308-4634-4

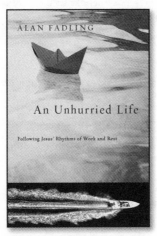

An Unhurried Life
978-0-8308-3573-7

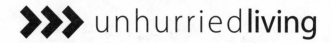

unhurried**living**

Many leaders feel hurried, and hurry is costing them more than they realize. Unhurried Living, founded by Alan & Gem Fadling, provides resources and training to help people learn to lead from fullness rather than leading on empty.

Great leadership begins on the inside, in your soul. Learning healthy patterns of rest and work can transform your leadership—your daily influence.

Built on more than twenty-five years of experience at the intersection of spiritual formation and leadership development, Unhurried Living seeks to inspire Christian leaders around the world to rest deeper so they can live fuller and lead better.

We seek to respond to questions many are asking:

Rest deeper: Why do I so often feel more drained than energized? Can I find space for my soul to breathe?

Live fuller: I have tried to fill my life with achievements, possessions and notoriety and I feel emptier than ever. Where can I find fullness that lasts?

Lead better: How can I step off the treadmill of mere busyness and make real, meaningful progress in my life and work?

Our purpose is to resource busy people so they can rediscover the genius of Jesus' unhurried way of life and leadership. We do this by…

Living all that we are learning so we share with others from experience and wisdom.

Developing digital, print and video content that encourages the practices of an unhurried life.

Training people in Jesus' unhurried way of living and leading.

Come visit us at unhurriedliving.com to discover free resources to help you

Rest Deeper. Live Fuller. Lead Better.

Web: unhurriedliving.com
Facebook: facebook.com/unhurriedliving
Twitter: UnhurriedLiving
Instagram: UnhurriedLiving
Email: info@unhurriedliving.com